WE BELONG DEAD

A Gay Perpective on the Classic Movie Monsters

DOUGLAS MCEWAN

Pulp Hero Press
The Most Dangerous Books on Earth
www.PulpHeroPress.com

© 2017 Douglas McEwan

No part of this publication may be reproduced, distributed, or transmitted in any form or by any means, including photocopying, recording, or other electronic or mechanical methods, without the prior written permission of the publisher, except for brief quotations embodied in critical reviews and certain other non-commercial uses permitted by copyright law.

Although every precaution has been taken to verify the accuracy of the information contained herein, no responsibility is assumed for any errors or omissions, and no liability is assumed for damages that may result from the use of this information.

The views expressed in this book are those of the author and do not necessarily reflect the views of Pulp Hero Press.

Pulp Hero Press publishes its books in a variety of print and electronic formats. Some content that appears in one format may not appear in another.

Portions of this book, in substantially altered form, were previously published in *The Q Guide to Classic Monster Movies*.

Editor: Bob McLain
Layout: Artisanal Text
ISBN 978-1-68390-065-8
Printed in the United States of America

Pulp Hero Press | www.PulpHeroPress.com
Address queries to bob@pulpheropress.com

This book is dedicated to the memory of three people who do not belong dead, but nonetheless are:

Dianne Jane Nobriga
(1950–1969)

David Edward Tarling
(1949–1988)

John Andrew Fugiel
(1953–1987)

I miss all of you. The party was just getting good when you left.

My candle burns at both ends,
It will not last the night,
But ah, my foes, and oh, my friends,
It gives a lovely light!
— Edna St. Vincent Millay

Yes. Go! You live! Go! You stay. We belong dead!
— The Frankenstein Monster (Boris Karloff)
demonstrating low self-esteem in *Bride of Frankenstein*

To die, to be really dead, that must be glorious.
— Count Dracula (Bela Lugosi)
expressing a minority opinion, in *Dracula*

I want to die. Only death can bring me release.
— Larry Talbot, aka the Wolfman (Lon Chaney Jr.)
explaining why he's a lousy date in *House of Frankenstein*

I want to live!
— Barbara Graham (Susan Hayward)
being far more upbeat on Death Row in *I Want to Live!*

For life is short but death is long, faro la faro li.
— Big Gypsy Singer (Adia Kuznetzoff)
singing a jolly song in *Frankenstein Meets the Wolfman*

*Just as soon as his problem's solved,
he'll be gay as a lark again. He's like that.*
— Elsa Von Frankenstein (Josephine Hutchinson),
a wife who apparently was not the last to know,
in *Son of Frankenstein*

CONTENTS

Introduction *Far Worse Things* ix

PART ONE
THE LIVING DEAD 1

Chapter 1 Bite Me! 3
Dracula

Chapter 2 The Vampire Idol 13
Bela Lugosi

Chapter 3 Children of the Night 17
Dracula's Brood

Chapter 4 Daddy's Little Ghoul 19
Dracula's Daughter

Chapter 5 Chip off the Old Stake 27
Son of Dracula

Chapter 6 House Parties 35
House of Frankenstein and *House of Dracula*

Chapter 7 Die, Mummy, Die! 43
The Mummy

Chapter 8 What's a Mummy to Do? 53
The Kharis Mummy Movies

Chapter 9 Two Zombies Straight Up 63
White Zombie and *I Walked with a Zombie*

The Living Dead Quiz 65

PART TWO
IT'S A MAD, MAD, MAD, MAD SCIENCE   67

Chapter 10   In the Beginning, Henry Created Man   69
Frankenstein

Chapter 11   The Mating Game   77
Bride of Frankenstein

Chapter 12   The King of Blood   87
Boris Karloff

Chapter 13   Sibling Rivalry   91
Son of Frankenstein

Chapter 14   Profaning His Name   101
The Frankenstein B-Movie Sequels

Chapter 15   All's Wells That Ends Wells   115
Two Very Mad Scientists from H.G. Wells

Chapter 16   Here's Looking at You, Kid   117
The Invisible Man

Chapter 17   No Man Is An…   125
Island of Lost Souls

Chapter 18   Bad, Science, Bad!   131
Some Other Notable Mad Scientists

The Mad Science Quiz   141

PART THREE
THE BEAST WITHIN 143

Chapter 19	The Doctor Will Kill You Now 145 *Doctors Jekyll and Misters Hyde*	
Chapter 20	Where Wolf? 149 *Werewolf of London*	
Chapter 21	A Dog's Life 153 *The Wolf Man*	
Chapter 22	Pussy Galore 159 *Cat People*	
Chapter 23	Family Dies 163 *The Chaneys*	
Chapter 24	Bad Moons Arisin' 167 *The Wolfman Sequels*	
	The Beast Within Quiz 175	
Epilogue	Who's on Last? 177 *Abbott & Costello Meet Frankenstein*	
Appendix	*Quiz Answers* 183	

About the Author 187

INTRODUCTION
Far Worse Things

There are far worse things awaiting man than death.
— Count Dracula (Bela Lugosi),
looking at the bright side in Dracula

I began watching the classic monster movies in 1962, right after I turned twelve years old, just as puberty began its playful dance through my body. Half a century ago we lived in a different world, especially if you were a teenager discovering you were gay. In movies and TV shows, homosexuality was never mentioned, did not exist. American society was in denial. The arbiters of taste and censorship believed that if it wasn't discussed, it would not exist. No gay news is good gay news. So it was underground, talked of only in schoolyard dirty jokes, often of enthusiastic viciousness.

"You're a queer" was the worst thing you could say to anyone. I know, because when I used the epithet on my younger brother one afternoon, having not the slightest idea what it actually meant, my mother basically exploded, and it was made abundantly clear to me that there was no worse thing I could say.

With the culture not explaining itself on the subject, and with my parents certainly unwilling to discuss such "disgusting matters," I was on my own to deal with the forbidden feelings I was developing. All I had were the old movies I watched on TV.

Of course, Laurel & Hardy, whom I'd always loved, shared beds rather a lot. Even when they were married to women, their primary partnership with each other trumped any romantic attachment. But they were prepared to discuss it only just so far. In their short *Their First Mistake*, in which they adopt a child together after Ollie's wife throws him out, Stan asks Ollie what her problem with their marriage was, and he answers, "She says I think more of you than I do of her."

"Well, you do, don't you?" asks Stan.

"We won't go into *that*," Ollie replies firmly, and that discussion is over.

On TV, Abbott & Costello shared not just an apartment, but its bedroom. Lou kept referring to zoftig Hillary Brooke as his "girlfriend," but she obviously, even to a kid viewer, held him in amused contempt and was clearly only humoring him. And as for The Three Stooges, well, that bizarre *ménage à trois* was far too S&M for my tastes anyway.

Movie homos were mostly Franklin Pangborn, Grady Sutton, and other comic sissies flouncing around W.C. Fields. The masculine W.C. was not the homophobe you'd think. When most studios declared Franklin Pangborn too overtly gay to be allowed in movies, Fields made a point of not only continuing to hire him but also to enlarge his roles. (Not all of the movie sissies were gay like Pangborn or Sutton. Bert Lahr played the biggest sissy in movie history, the Cowardly Lion, but off stage or screen, he was long married with two kids. His son is a first-rate theater writer whose books I love.) Often, movie homos were silky, effeminate, sinister types, like Peter Lorre in *The Maltese Falcon*, who will shoot you if you let them, but who are disarmed easily and exist primarily as punching bags for Humphrey Bogart to show what a man he is.

But just as I was reaching the point where I was seriously drawn to other males in a way I was not drawn to girls, and as some of my young male friends and I began *touching* each other and *exploring* each other in deepest secret because we knew it was *wrong* (we were dabbling in sex acts man was meant to leave alone), I began watching the monsters Universal Studios had unleashed on the world, and I began making an emotional connection.

From the things I heard from grown-ups, like my parents, I knew that what I was doing, and the even worse things I wanted to do, were monstrous. Dad used that word freely in describing "perverts," never knowing he was talking to me about me. I was getting the unsent message: I was a monster. And so I began to identify with the monsters. You should have

INTRODUCTION: FAR WORSE THINGS

seen me, stalking about the wooded area near our house in a black Dracula cape my mother had made for me out of an old black skirt of hers.

The interpretations I shall make at length in this book of what the monster movies mean are not what they mean, they're what they meant to me.

Count Dracula wasn't gay, though in Universal's famous 1931 movie, Bela Lugosi warns off his female roommates and sucks the brains out of Renfield. And he has a daughter, and later, Lon Chaney's son.

Baron Frankenstein wasn't gay. He has a fiancée he avoids, who later becomes his bride, whom he leaves in their wedding bed while he wanders off into the night with Dr. Pretorius, who most definitely *was* gay, *really, really* gay. And Henry Frankenstein had a variety of sons, created in both conventional and unconventional manners.

Lawrence Talbot wasn't gay. In fact, in *The Wolfman*, he's something of a wolf before he ever acquires his curse. He even peeps on Evelyn Ankers in her bedroom using an enormous telescope intended for studying the stars—celestial stars, not movie stars.

Henry Jekyll wasn't gay. He was engaged to Lana Turner, something most gay men would know better than to be, and as Hyde, he fixates on beautiful Ingrid Bergman (understandable; if she's good enough to obsess Alfred Hitchcock, she's good enough to obsess Henry Jekyll), and makes her life unbearable, the way straight guys do, and is clearly having as much of an affair with her as the combined Puritanism of Louis B. Mayer, Will Hayes, and Joseph Breen would allow.

The monsters weren't gay—except, of course, they were.

The monsters weren't intended to be homosexuals, except possibly when James Whale was behind the lens, but for me and my fellow queer youth growing up in the gay-intolerant era of the mid-20th century, these monsters spoke to our lives. That they flourished in marvelous gothic fantasy films, some brilliant, most ridiculous, all imagination-stirring, only made them more special.

Hollywood's message may have seemed clear: you're gay; you're a monster. The villagers must hunt you down and destroy you. However, there was a more subversive underside to them. Almost without exception the monsters are presented sympathetically. Oh, Henry Jekyll was a hypocritical bastard and I wouldn't want to pal around with Dorian Gray, but Frankenstein's monster was a lonely innocent, persecuted for existing, good with children—some of the time. The Wolfman was an heroic fellow who'd acquired a cursed life when he came to the aid of a damsel in distress. Even souless Dracula is often presented as a lonely, isolated figure, removed from humanity, burdened by a curse acquired in defense of his country. The villagers are usually frightened, ignorant yahoos, with a hair-trigger lynch-mob response to most any stimulus.

These movies said to me: it is intolerant society that is wrong. Hang in there, fight the good fight. If you get enough sequels, eventually everyone will love you. The monsters will become *The Munsters*. Once Abbott & Costello show up, you're home free.

There is hope.

So if you ever felt like you turned into a monster on full moons and prowled the streets to find fresh meat to feed your unspeakable hunger, if you ever felt a forbidden thirst, if you ever watched Frankenstein's monster hounded by ignorant torch-bearing peasants and felt, "You and me both, Frankie," or if you ever watched Vincent Price wander the cobwebbed corridors of a moldering mansion late at night and thought to yourself, "I *want* that dressing gown," this may be the right book for you.

So come on in. Stay close to the candles; the stairway can be treacherous. And whatever you do, *don't open that door before sunrise*! Let's hope we don't have to delve into Matters Man Was Meant to Leave Alone.

Drat! We do.

PART ONE
The Living Dead

He's just resting, waiting for a new life to come.
— Henry Frankenstein (Colin Clive) in *Frankenstein*

What's the worst thing about life? Death, the big bugaboo, the terrible irony that we live and learn for a few brief seconds between endless gulfs of oblivion. And death is the great topic of horror movies, with sex running a close second. Thus it is not surprising that we find an awful lot of the living dead in horror movies.

Let's take vampires. Over the last decade, they've replaced high-school dances and football games as the number one TV teenager romantic occupation. If you're dating a living boy friend, you are so last century. There's a lot that's attractive about the vampire state. First off, you live on, century after century. None of this death and oblivion crap. The hours are great. Nice clothes. Optional characteristics include super-strength, the ability to turn into a bat or a wolf or a mist, the ability to control the minds of others, and you get younger-looking when you're well fed. The number of people I know who would embrace vampirism in a heartbeat just to stay youthful is huge. And the liquid diet keeps you thin.

There are drawbacks. The worst is no sex. I'm sorry, they're dead. The sex is all metaphoric. The lesser drawback is that you have to kill people to live. Then there's that liquid diet again. No steak, eggs, and chocolate.

And of course, there's always annoying Van Helsings, or more recently, Buffys, around trying to kill you. But overall, what is worse, dying of a heart attack at 72 or being staked by Van Helsing sat age 548? It may be a "loathsome existence," as vampire hunters always maintain, but how else can you see the movies that will come out in 2117? They'll be *awesome*!

We all know who the king vampire is. Count Vlad Dacula, late of Transylvania. Let's look at some Dracula movies.

1

BITE ME!
Dracula (1931)

> *The spider spinning his web for the unwary fly. The blood is the life, Mr. Renfield.*
> — Count Dracula (Bela Lugosi), explaining his entire *modus operandi* to an unwary Renfield

For millions of people, when they hear the opening strains of Tchaikovsky's *Scene from Swan Lake*, their minds are not filled with swans on a lake, ballerinas in tutus, or, more recently, Matthew Bourne's gorgeous bare-chested men with feathered legs, but rather with bats, wolves, and Bela Lugosi, because, over eighty years ago, someone at Universal Studios, probably not uninvolved director Tod Browning, decided that it was a nicely sinister sounding piece of public domain music to run under the opening credits of their shaggy-bat release *Dracula*, the very first American sound monster movie.

The Story

Gay real estate agent R. Renfield, ignoring the advice of primitive peasants, travels to the castle of elderly (about 400 years) Count Dracula in the Carpathian mountains of Transylvania to handle the details of Dracula's move to England, only to get seduced and sucked by the ancient predator. Dracula and now-insane Renfield travel to England, where Renfield is committed to an insane asylum while Dracula bites his way through the female cast, until crusty Professor Van Helsing pounds a phallic stake through his heart and peace is re-established, at least until the sequel.

THE OTHER *DRACULA*

Made at the same time as *Dracula* was *Drácula*, Universal's Spanish-language version, shot on the same sets, using the same script, but with a director, George Melford, who didn't speak Spanish but who wanted to show the world he was a *director*. Both films are available on the same DVD or Blu-ray, and they make a fascinating comparison. The Spanish *Drácula* is vastly better, despite being weighed down with an actor playing *Conde Drácula*, Carlos Villarías, who made Lugosi look like a master of subtlety and nuance.

It wasn't the script. It was the same script Tod Browning's assistants were filming. The pacing can't be credited with the improvement; the Spanish *Drácula* is half an hour *longer* than the English-language one. Nor, as implied above, is it the acting—though the Spanish Renfield, Pablo Ivarez Rubio, gives a fascinating performance, and the heroine, "Eva," is played by Lupita Tovar as a sexy young minx who puts Helen Chandler deeply in the shade. Tovar, who married *Drácula*'s producer, Paul Kohner, passed away in November of 2016, at the age of 106!

It's the camera, which moves about, finding us more interesting stuff to look at. It's the more-interesting lighting. It's the eerier effects. In the last analysis, it's a director who cared about what he was doing.

Tovar testified that the cast and crew looked at Browning's rushes each day and decided to prove they could do it better. They did.

The Production

Carl Laemmle Jr., son of Universal Studios founder Carl Laemmle, was in the audience the night Bela Lugosi opened on Broadway in his stage version of *Dracula*. Little Carl immediately began pressuring Daddy to buy the film rights. Big Carl (Actually, both men were quite short) may have felt *Dracula* was beneath him, but its enormous financial success on the stages of London and Broadway was not.

Universal planned to star Lon Chaney as Count Dracula. Tod Browning, Lon's most-favored director, with whom he had made such silent classics as *The Unholy Three*, *The Unknown*, and *London After Midnight*, came attached. Lon died shortly before *Dracula* was to be made. Browning didn't.

Conrad Veidt was the preferred second choice, and one salivates at the thought of how wonderful he could have been in the role (he was truly better suited to the role than Lugosi, as well as a better actor), but he'd retreated back to Germany, afraid his poor command of English would hurt his career in America. (A fear Lugosi never shared.) Eventually, Universal did the obvious thing, and gave the role to the man who had set Broadway ablaze in the part, and created, in the process, the first official horror star, Bela Lugosi.

What's Good About It

Not much, really. It gives us our first-ever glimpse of Universal's evil Neverland, its fairy-tale anti-Oz, where the forthcoming decade and a half of scary movies would be set. Castle Dracula looks wonderful. I want to move in today. (There is one exterior shot of it that looks nothing like the other exterior shots, being in an entirely different color and architectural style, and we're just supposed to ignore the grossly mis-matched shot.) Inside it is a gothic wet dream of a spooky ruin. This vast, fabulous set, with its giant staircase, its enormous spider-web, and a tree growing in through an immense shattered window, gets slightly less than three minutes of screen time. (It reappears four years later in *Dracula's Daughter*.) We will eventually stare at Dr. Seward's boring drawing room for what seems like hours, but we get just three minutes in this great set.

The first 21 minutes, though slowly paced, look great, and have a really wonderful spooky atmosphere. But after 21 minutes we come to...

What's Bad About It

Of all the American films ever to have achieved the status of Beloved Classic Movie, *Dracula* is without doubt the worst, a dull, stagy, static bore. Once the action catches up to the Broadway play, abandon hope all ye who remain awake.

Bela Lugosi's performance is static and slow to the point of being dreary, though there's no mistaking his magnetism either, and the halting, unfamiliar delivery is very appropriate for a four-hundred-year-old feudal lord who has learned English from books. If he lacks the feral menace others have brought to Dracula, he still has a weird otherworldliness that befits the character. And he stamped it so indelibly that even today, when we have had much better Draculas from much better actors, many still consider him the gold standard. I can't say with honesty that he is good in *Dracula*, but he isn't terrible. And whatever he was, he was not what was wrong with *Dracula*.

I don't know what director Tod Browning was doing while his assistants made this movie. Maybe he was depressed by the recent death of his favorite collaborator and friend, Lon Chaney. Maybe he was drunk. Maybe he was bored. Whatever he was, he was not engaged in movie-making. I've seen movies he made where he *was* engaged, firing on all cylinders, movies like *The Unholy Three* (silent version), the unforgettable *Freaks*, and especially the riveting and gripping silent *The Unknown*. These movies are terrific and terrifying. There is none of the desultory slackness of *Dracula*. The man had talent. Where was it during *Dracula*? Even the great Sir Alfred Hitchcock made some dull, bum movies, as anyone who has sat through such tedious bores as *Topaz, Torn Curtain, I Confess,* and *The Paradine Case* can attest. But even in those turkeys, you can see where Hitch was trying to make a good movie, applying his talent and his art. But where the Tod Browning of *Freaks* and *The Unknown* was during the filming of *Dracula* is a mystery.

Garrett Fort's screenplay for *Dracula* is often faulted for relying too much upon the stage play. Yes, the movie has a lot of people standing around drawing rooms talking, but there are lots of movies of people hanging around rooms talking that are brilliant. *My Dinner with Andre* is a critic's darling, and it's just two guys siting in a restaurant bullshitting. The early portions of *My Dinner with Andre* are wonderful, and if I ever manage to stay awake through the entire film (I've tried three times without success), I'm sure I'll see that the critics are right.

In *Dracula*, the camera just sits there a great deal of the time, watching the cast talk in endless medium shots, without a close up or a change of angle to wake us up.

And the film is afraid to be shocking. There's a very famous scene in the novel *Dracula* where Dracula slices open his own chest and forces Mina to drink the blood that gushes from the wound. It's a graphic, unforgettable image of oral sex as blood drinking. In the movie, Mina, played by Helen Chandler as a limp, listless dishrag, whom Pauline Kael rightly points out is "too anemic to attract a vampire," confesses what Dracula has done to her. "He came to me. He opened a vein in his arm and he made me drink," all sobbed out so unintelligibly that you're lucky even to make out her words. It has nothing like the impact of the book's image of Mina with her head held against her will to Dracula's breast, to suckle his blood.

The climax of *Dracula* is one of the biggest movie let-downs of all time. Renfield, played by Dwight Frye with a manic gusto, drops in for no reason at Carfax Abbey, Draculas' London/Whitby digs. (The movie seems to believe that Whitby is a suburb of London, with Dracula commuting between them via batwing each night. Whitby is two hundred sixty-four miles from London as the bat flies. That's a hell of a long flap.) Van Helsing, played boringly with an astonishing degree of stolid pompous blather by Edward Van Sloan (also a veteran of the Broadway production), and "romantic" lead Jonathan Harker, played with an impressive lack of masculinity by never-married David Manners, also wander by for no reason. Dracula and Mina stroll in via a different route. This momentary, arbitrary, coincidental convergence takes the place of Bram Stoker's climactic trans-European chase by boat, train, and horseback, complete with a gun battle with a band of gypsies in Dracula's employ. Five people wander aimlessly into the same house.

Much better than a big chase. Well, cheaper anyway. (David Manners, no fool, lived well into his nineties without ever once viewing *Dracula*. Whenever a film historian interviewed him, they invariably offered to show him *Dracula*, and he always turned them down.)

Not having a stake, Van Helsing hammers a wooden slat through Dracula—*off screen!* We hear a groan. That's it. I'm so scared. Anyway, it's over. Some chimes chime, probably to wake the audience up.

What's Gay About It

The book, and consequently the film, is all about how becoming sexually aroused makes you evil. It's Victorianism distilled. Sex is evil. And for me, it was gay sex is evil.

Dracula has prepared a suite for Renfield that is clean, neat, and huge, with supper laid out. (Dracula has no servants, and I doubt that he got the female vampires to clean the room and cook the food, so he must have done it himself. I love the mental image of this domestic Dracula playing housemaid and cooking a meal he can never taste. However, the mental image of him preparing the drugged wine for Renfield I can easily credit.) But Renfield won't be having dinner. He's going to *be* dinner. Date rape is high on Dracula's agenda and, with the memorable excuse of "I never drink wine," he slips Renfield a rufie.

Renfield passes out, and Dracula's harem of brides (no wonder he never drinks wine; Dracula's a Mormon!) move in on him, but Dracula banishes his bitches with a stern gesture, sinks down on Renfield's prone young body himself, and starts sucking away. If they moved the setting forward a century, I'd have to assume Renfield and Dracula met on the internet. Dracula probably lied about his age. (Actually, given Dracula is over four hundred years old, his just being alive constitutes lying about his age.)

Gay sex with a man old enough to be his distant ancestor leaves Renfield broken mentally, and has turned him into a major submissive. He spends the rest of the movie insanely devoted to Dracula with a manic passion. When Van Helsing tries holding hands with Renfield in the asylum, Renfield snatches his hand away, shouting, "Keep your filthy hands to yourself!" Renfield only has eyes for the Master. He knows what Seward's sanatorium really is: one of those clinics that "cures" gay people.

Sobbing alone in his cell, Renfield hears Vlad howling in wolf form below his window and chats with him through the bars. Vlad is apparently sending orders telepathically, but Renfield has to reply aloud. "No, Master, please! Please don't ask me to do that! Don't! Not *her*!" Renfield wants no part of heterosex. It's an interesting concept; a sadist-master ordering his masochist-slave to have straight sex because that's what he hates most.

Certainly the sexual aggression of pounding a phallic stake through another person is hard to miss. Basically, the whole movie is about reanimated corpses raping the living. Gay necrophilia. There will be more than enough of that in the movies to come. But then, how much necrophilia is *enough*, anyway?

Aftermath

Opening on St. Valentine's Day, as befits this tender tale of a gay corpse raping the living, with the blatant giveaway advertising slogan on its posters of "The Strangest Passion the World Has Ever Known," *Dracula* was a huge, studio-saving hit, one of the highest-grossing movies of 1931. The Carls got the message. *Frankenstein* was greenlit, *Dracula* would spawn five sequels, and the horror boom of the 1930s was off and flapping. The aftermath was really the rest of this book.

And the movies could only get better.

STILL STANDING

"Oh, Briggs," says Van Helsing, summoning Mina's nurse some fifty-four minutes into the film. Watching this movie at age 12, I would get terribly excited when Briggs arrived.

You see, back in 1962, shortly after I first saw *Dracula*, a very close friend of mine from school, still my friend today, had a blessed event in his family. His mother had a baby. No, no, that wasn't the blessed event. They hired a nurse to care for the child in its first few months, and that nurse was named Joan Standing. Before being a real nurse, she had been a movie actress, and she had played Briggs, Mina's nurse, in *Dracula*.

There she was in my friend's house *every day*, and she was in *Dracula! The Dracula!* She had known Bela Lugosi! He had even put the whammy on her in a later scene. No, she wasn't famous or rich, but *she was in Dracula!* She was officially the coolest person I knew.

So whenever I could be, I was underfoot at my friend's house, asking questions, begging for stories, drinking in just being in the same room with her. Tell me! Tell me! Share the unsharable experience! You were there, in Universal's magical fairy-tale horror-movie land. What was it like? What was *he* like?

And so she told me. She told me how Bela didn't know English, and learned his lines phonetically, off a chalkboard. (That explains a lot about his weird cadences and his career-long tendency to emphasize the wrong syllables in words and the wrong words in sentences.) How he was courtly and gentlemanly with women. How, when she got married, during the production of *Dracula*, he bought her one of the peasant women's outfits from the early scenes of the movie as a wedding gift. She did not tell me what Tod Browning was doing instead of directing the film, but she did tell me that Dwight Frye was charming and funny.

Joan died in 1979. And were she still alive, as I type this she'd be 112. She made sixty-two movies. One of her films was a silent version of Dickens's *Oliver Twist* with Jackie Coogan in the title role and Lon Chaney as Fagin. (I wish I'd known that then. I'd have peppered her with questions about Chaney.) She was in a early talkie version of *Jane Eyre* with Colin Clive as Mr. Rochester. (Had I known that then, I'd have been full of questions about Clive as well.) Her last movie was a bloody terrible movie, *Lil Abner* (which wastes Buster Keaton in a small role). But does it matter what else she had been in? She was in *Dracula*! She was an immortal! She was a *goddess*! And she was changing my friend's baby brother's diapers.

Whenever I look at *Dracula*, there she is, unmistakable and easily recognizable. There she is on my TV screen, freeze-framed, at this very moment. Hi, Joan. Thank you for putting up with me so patiently. I'll never forget you. For one brief year in my youth, you were the coolest person I knew. You knew Count Dracula personally.

Wow.

2

THE VAMPIRE IDOL
Bela Lugosi (1882–1956)

On October 20, 1882, Bela Ferenc Dezső Blaskó was born in Lugoj (pronounced "Lugosh"), Hungary. On February 14, 1931, having dropped most of his American-movie-publicity-unfriendly names, and replacing them with a mild corruption of the name of his birthplace, "Bela Lugosi" became a movie star.

Bela was the youngest of four children. A strong-willed son of a strong-willed father, Bela left home at the age of 12. Unable to get an acting career rolling at 12, Bela became one of the many minor miners no sensible economy is without. Eight years after leaving home, he made his stage debut.

For the next two decades, Bela played hundreds of different roles on stage, including his favorite one to mention when he became an American movie star, Jesus Christ. The existing photographs of Bela as Jesus show us what looks like Dracula in a hippie phase, showing enough manflesh to raise less-than-holy thoughts in his female and gay male public. He appeared in various roles in a lot of Shakespeare's plays, albeit, translated into Hungarian, which I'm sure improves them greatly.

We are told that Lugosi was a much-admired actor, though we were mostly told this by Bela. He did become a member of Hungary's National Theater, though not in leads. He enlisted in the army during World War I. Bela was fond of telling gullible publicists in Hollywood that he had been a hangman in the army, though no proof of his grisly occupation survives, if it ever existed at all.

After the war, Bela aligned himself with a revolutionary movement. When the revolution failed, he was declared a traitor and fled to Vienna, a political refugee. He emigrated to America in 1921. By the time he was cast as Count Dracula on Broadway in 1927, he had still not learned English, and was memorizing dialogue phonetically, but even after he had finally learned the language, his trademark overplaying never lessened.

Bela still has many fans and devotees, people who believe he was a great actor. I am not among them. However, even at his worst he was enjoyable, and no one can deny the indefinable charm that existed between him and the camera he seldom held back for.

His Count Dracula is so on the nose vocally, and one of his most underplayed roles, that it comes off fairly well, both in *Dracula* and even better in *Abbott & Costello Meet Frankenstein*. But as early as his first starring role after *Dracula*, Dr. Mirakle in *Murders in the Rue Morgue*, he is in the full flower of the wild overacting that sadly became his real trademark. It lost him his Universal contract. Barely a year after *Dracula*, he was appearing in cheap serials and low-budget programmers like *White Zombie*.

Lugosi got the occasional non-horror role, such as small parts as Russians in W.C. Fields' *International House* and Garbo's *Ninotchka*. No one left the theater discussing his performances in those movies, but perhaps that was a good thing.

They did leave the theater discussing his performance in *Son of Frankenstein*, as the broken-necked shepherd/graverobber Ygor. It may be his finest performance in a movie. He's unrecognizable, either visually or audibly; his performance is big and broad, without being *too* big and broad, and his relationship with the monster is genuinely touching.

But by the 1940s, the use of him in *The Wolfman* is more typical, slipped into a five-minute role, strictly to put his name into the credits. His Abbott & Costello romp in 1948 was his last major studio motion picture. The degradations of *Old Mother Riley Meets the Vampire, Bela Lugosi Meets a Brooklyn Gorilla*, and the trash of Ed Wood lay not far ahead.

Bela arrived at Universal for *Dracula* with three short marriages already behind him; their quick terminations generally ascribed to his jealousy. The love of his life was clearly his fourth wife, Lillian, the mother of his only child, Bela Jr. But even Lillian eventually couldn't take his dark moods as his career sank and his tragic morphine addiction rose, so she divorced Bela and later married Brian Donlevy.

Bela, like many another star from Peter Lorre to Judy Garland, became hooked on painkillers prescribed by studio Dr. Feelgoods. It is to his everlasting credit that he not only triumphed over his addiction, but became the first Hollywood star ever to go public with his rehab.

Sadly, the rigors of detoxing took their toll on the elderly, frail actor, and he lived only a few months longer. His pathetic last marriage was to a fan named Hope, but she was really His Last Hope. She wanted Dracula, but what she got was a very old, weak, washed-up, foul-tempered former star, and rather than being touched by his plight and giving him the gift of a final sustaining love, she took out her disappointment and disillusionment on him.

His sad final months came to a quiet end when his heart simply stopped beating while he slept on August 16, 1956, in his home in Hollywood. He was, supposedly according to his wishes, buried in one of his Dracula capes.

Bela would be surprised and pleased to learn he is not only still remembered but that he still has thousands of fans. He has indeed become immortal.

3

CHILDREN OF THE NIGHT
Dracula's Brood

Kids! What the hell is wrong with these kids today?
— Lyrics by Lee Adams from "*Kids*," in *Bye Bye, Birdie*

Dracula differs from our other evil friends, Frankenstein's monster, Larry Talbot, Imhoptep, Edward Hyde, etc., in that he actually existed. Oh, he wasn't a vampire and he didn't live for 400 years, nor was he known to wear opera cloaks, but he ruled parts of what is now Romania for three brief spans back in the 15th century.

Frankly, if I had the choice of falling prey to the movie's Count Dracula or the real Vlad Dracula, aka Vlad the Impaler, I'd take the movie vampire any day. The real guy was *very* strict, and believed in vigorous and creative forms of grotesquely unpleasant corporal punishment.

In both real life and reel life, Dracula was a breeder. Nasty old Vlad had three sons, while Universal's Count Dracula had a daughter and a son. Let's look at these family portraits.

4

DADDY'S LITTLE GHOUL
Dracula's Daughter (1936)

> *She was beautiful when she died, a hundred years ago.*
> — Von Helsing (Edward Van Sloan),
> displaying more knowledge than he actually has

The Story

Seconds after *Dracula* ends, Van Helsing, now pointlessly renamed *Von* Helsing, is arrested for the murder of Count Dracula. All the other characters from *Dracula* who could explain why he did it have apparently vanished from the earth. For no reason, Von Helsing enlists a psychiatrist, Dr. Garth, to defend him instead of a lawyer. The case against him falls apart when Countess Marya Zeleska, the daughter of Count Dracula, arrives and steals her father's corpse (the bat hasn't fallen far from the belfry), which she cremates in an attempt to exorcize the curse of vampirism from her family. When this fails, she implores Dr. Garth to help cure her. He mistakenly thinks she's merely insane. She then develops an unfathomable crush on the unappetizing shrink, and kidnaps his shrewish girlfriend, to force him to follow her back to Transylvania. There, her jealous, evil sidekick, Sandor, kills her with a wooden arrow.

The Production

Today, when our multiplexes are cluttered with almost nothing but sequels, prequels, reboots, and re-imaginings, it may seem surprising to learn that the Laemmles were not sequel-happy. In their entire reign over Universal, they produced only two horror sequels, *Bride of Frankenstein* and *Dracula's Daughter*. Five years elapsed between *Dracula* and *Dracula's Daughter*, and between those films lay the whole of the Laemmle's horror output, for *Dracula* was their first gothic (if you don't count their 1925 silent *The Phantom of the Opera*) and *Dracula's Daughter* was their last, released two months after the Laemmles had sold the studio.

The direction was handled by Lambert Hillyer, a veteran of dozens of westerns, who had just done the Karloff-Lugosi science fiction thriller *The Invisible Ray*. Yes, the perfect man to handle a moody supernatural thriller about a vampire lesbian trying to go straight was a man who made Tom Mix shoot-em-ups.

Edward Van Sloan returned to the role of "Von" Helsing, bringing his same lack of magic to the role. Countess Marya Zeleska is lovely Gloria Holden, a felicitous piece of casting. She's wonderful in the part. Countess Zeleska's sinister sidekick and amanuensis Sandor is played by Irving Pichel, with hair like Alfalfa of *Our Gang*, greased down, parted in the center, and wearing more make-up than the countess. Our romantic leads, Dr. Garth and his "assistant" Janet Blake, are played by the excellent actor Otto Kruger and the lovely Marguerite Churchill. Vile gossip maven Hedda Hopper shows up in a tiny role as a socialite hostess. Dracula is played by a stuffed dummy wearing what looks like a wax Lugosi mask, who gives a more restrained performance than Bela was likely to have given.

Since Lugosi was originally contracted to appear in the film but was let go when his role was reduced to lying down and being burned, he was paid $4000 for doing nothing whatsoever. Ironically, he was better paid here than he had been on *Dracula*.

What's Good About It

Quite a bit. It's certainly an improvement on *Dracula*. It's better paced, it has a few effectively moody scenes, particularly the one of Zeleska cremating her dad's effigy in a spooky, foggy hollow that has that glorious gothic look I treasure. During the ceremony, Countess Zeleska holds, but can not behold, a crude wooden crucifix as she exorcizes the curse from her father.

There are some wonderful sets. The opening scene, which is supposed to be the cellar of Carfax Abby, is actually a slight redress of the entryway to Baron Frankenstein's laboratory from *Bride of Frankenstein*, shot just a few weeks earlier. The great Castle Dracula main hall set, complete with cobwebs and the tree sticking in through the window, makes a brief reappearance near the end.

The best things about the film are the performances of Gloria Holden and Irving Pichel. She is eerie, sexy, and solemn, and vacillates well between good and evil. She is beautiful yet creepy, and her look is *the* classic female vampire look perfected.

Pichel speaks in a *deep*, sepulcher-like voice, always slowly and with maximum sinister intonation. If he was the voice of the telephone time clock, it would always be *too late!* Irving Pichel was mostly a director. For Merian C. Cooper he co-directed *The Most Dangerous Game*, and, the same year as his appearance as Sandor, he co-directed *SHE*, perhaps the campiest film of the entire 1930s. Later, he directed *Destination Moon* for charming George Pal. Two other important acting roles played by Pichel always spring to my mind: Cary Grant's defense attorney when Mae West sues Grant in the glorious comic romp *I'm No Angel*, and the tender, restrained, unsinister voice of the grown-up Roddy McDowell in John Ford's magnificent *How Green Was My Valley*.

There's a superb scene where Zeleska sits at her piano, trying to play sweet music, but with Sandor's sinister verbal interjections forcing her into a minor key, playing music only that the drinking of human blood can assuage. (I have CDs like that; don't you?) Sandor's baleful kibitzing also causes an unseen orchestra to begin accompanying her, so that when she stops playing, the music continues on its own until she orders it to "*Stop! Stop! STOP!*"

What's Bad About It

Dr. Garth and his "assistant," Janet Blake, our bickering, bantering romantic leads. Garth is supposed to be handsome, charming, and witty. Janet is supposed to be beautiful, charming, playful, and funny. Together they are supposed to have that we're-bickering-because-we-don't-know-we're-really-madly-in-love-with-each-other chemistry, and their scenes together are meant to be Noel Coward-funny. Well, she is beautiful. One out of nine ain't bad.

Kruger was 50, and never handsome, sexy, nor charming. As cantankerous wealthy older men making their heirs jump through hoops in *Perry Mason* episodes in the 1950s, he was fine. As a romantic leading man and a master of witty repartee, he is not. The first actor hired for the role was the suave, handsome, possibly gay actor Cesar Romero. He would have been sexier, funnier, and more charming, but a Latin doctor in London might have been hard to explain. Kruger was at least convincingly English.

Marguerite Churchill, as Janet Blake, is pretty, but her role is extremely annoying. When Marya says "I am Dracula's daughter," it's almost a surprise. You'd think Dracula's daughter would be Churchill, since she sucks the life out of every scene she's in. She and Kruger have no chemistry. Their would-be comic banter sinks every scene it befouls deeper than the Lost Continent of Atlantis.

Much of the plot makes no sense. Having Von Helsing accused of murdering Count Dracula makes for a clever story hook. But, sadly, that plotline just peters out after Dracula's corpse is stolen. Von Helsing *insists* on using Dr. Garth as his defense attorney despite the fact that Garth isn't a lawyer. Garth, being a psychiatrist, naturally assumes that Von Helsing is insane. Given that Von Helsing has hired a doctor for a defense lawyer, and his legal defense is that "you can't murder a man who's been dead for five centuries," Garth has a point.

Garth becomes involved with both Von Helsing and Countess Zeleska by coincidence. The Countess explains her problem to Dr. Garth, that "someone, something...reaches out from beyond the grave and fills me with horrible impulses." Garth, who thinks she's insane, disastrously recommends that she set whatever tempts her in front of herself and then resist it. He promises to help her do it, and then immediately leaves her on her own. Bad doctor, bad!

What's Gay About It

Ironically, it was the two sequels, *Bride of Frankenstein* and *Dracula's Daughter*, which tried so hard to make breeders of the monsters, that turned out to be two of the more overtly gay of the Laemmle horrors. The notorious Sapphic seduction scene of *Dracula's Daughter* earned it a place in the hearts of generations of lesbians.

Marya is a classic repressed gay character, a vampire lesbian who craves to be normal and seeks a psychiatrist to cure her of her lesbianic vampirism, with his scientific behavior modification and his manly hetero butchness.

Sandor is a gay enabler. He knows that Dr. Garth's I-can-make-you-straight therapy is a crock, and that Marya can only find true happiness by embracing her inner vampire lesbian, which is best accomplished by embracing someone else.

Her lament is all-too-familiar to any of us that have listened to the self-delusions of pathetic "ex-gays," touting their hard-won ersatz normalcy. "I can live a normal life now," she says to Sandor, "think normal things, even play normal music again." No more Broadway show tunes for Countess Marya.

One of her victims is a big poncy pouf in a top hat, tails, ascot, and effeminate penciled eyebrows, but her most notorious victim is in the Big Scene. Lovely Nan Grey, who would quickly rise to more important roles, plays a girl who walks the streets at night but isn't a prostitute because this is 1936 and the Hays Office says there's no such thing. Vampires are real, but whores are a myth. She wanders out on a bridge, clearly suicidal. Sandor, lurking in the fog, a craft at which he has Olympic-level skills, steps out and tempts her with an offer to pose for an artist. Lily, appropriately named for the flower of death, agrees to do it.

Marya is at first disappointed in Lily. "You have beautiful hands, but they're so white and bloodless." She's a white lily. Deciding that a pale, bloodless girl is a good first temptation—baby steps—Marya plays out a classic lesbian vampire seduction, quickly getting Lily out of her blouse and her bra straps down. Lily's pulsating aorta proves too much for Marya's very limited self-control, particularly when handed straight lines on a platter:

Lily: "Why are you looking at me that way? Won't I do?"
Marya: "Yes, you'll do very well indeed."

Late in the picture, at the castle, Marya has been having some success resisting the urge to dine on Janet, but she's weakening fast. She's only inhuman after all. To save Janet (why?) from Marya, Garth agrees to become her undead boyfriend, and teach her the Jedi ways of heterosex, deciding that eternal life with a hot babe who desires him is a price he's willing to pay to save the woman the script says he loves. Big of him. But just as she is preparing to sink her fangs in Garth's less-than-savory throat, Sandor's jealousy gets the better of him, and he shoots a wooden arow into the poor old vampiress. Drat!

Aftermath

The Laemmles had lost the studio by the time *Dracula's Daughter* opened. The new regime wanted to leave the horror business behind, so the Dracula franchise would lie dormant for seven years, before Marya's little brother would terrorize the screen.

A CONUNDRUM

The last lines of *Dracula's Daughter* present a puzzle to the horror logician:

Sir Basil: "The woman is beautiful." (No, that's not the conundrum.)

Von Helsing: "She was beautiful when she died, a hundred years ago."

She died *one* hundred years ago? Excuse me? Dracula has been dead since 1476. That was 460 years before the *circa*-1936 setting of *Dracula's Daughter*. Once converted to vampires, the undead can *not* sire children. I'm sorry, but those are the rules.

Therefore, Marya Zeleska *nee* Dracula can not have been born later than 1477. She appears to have died no later than age 40, let's say around 1516. That would mean she died no later than around 420 years earlier than when Von Helsing makes his one hundred years estimate. We are repeatedly told that Von Helsing is a great scientist. Perhaps, but he's no mathematician. The one thing we can say with certainty about this horror lesbian classic is things don't add up.

5

CHIP OFF THE OLD STAKE
Son of Dracula (1943)

> *I am Count Alucard. Announce me!*
> — Count Alucard, aka Count Dracula Jr.
> (Lon Chaney Jr.), late for the party

The Story

At Dark Oaks, a plantation somewhere deep in the American South, a party is being thrown by the Caldwell sisters, cheery blonde Claire and morbid brunette Kay, to welcome Count Alucard, a Hungarian nobleman Kay met in Europe. Alucard is a no-show, but arrives after the festivities, killing Colonel Caldwell, the sister's elderly father, by drinking all of his blood, though there were leftover refreshments. The colonel's new will leaves all of his money to Claire and the plantation to Kay.

Kay then shocks her fiancé, Frank Stanley, by eloping with Alucard. Frank confronts Alucard and shoots him, but the bullet passes through him harmlessly and kills Kay, cowering behind him. Frank confesses to the sheriff. Now a vampire, Kay appears to Frank in his cell, revealing that Alucard is Count Dracula Jr. Kay tells Frank to kill him, so that Frank and Kay can live together eternally as immortal vampires. Kay releases Frank from his cell and he kills Alucard by burning his coffin, so the rising rays of the sun destroy him. But then Frank double-crosses Kay, burning her to death and eradicating the curse of vampirism from America.

The Production

According to the *fascinating* autobiography of novelist and screenwriter Curt Siodmak, *Wolf Man's Maker*, much as his brother, *film noir* director Robert Siodmak, and he loved each other personally, professionally they had a world-class case of sibling rivalry.

Curt had written *Son of Dracula* and a director was needed. Curt had been supporting his brother, since Robert had been fired from Paramount for publically referring to his product there as "Paramount shit," so Curt recommended to Universal that they assign the movie to Robert. They did. Come Robert's first day on the picture, he fired Curt, who had gotten him the job. With siblings like these making the movie, is it any wonder that *Son of Dracula* is, at heart, the story of two siblings, one nice and one nasty, who come to different ends?

The Universal brass of 1943 cast Lon Chaney Jr. as their vampire. If they weren't all dead, I'd want to slap them.

Kindly family friend and nosy control freak Dr. Brewster is played by Frank Craven, who had played, both on Broadway and in the movie, the narrator role of the "Stage Manager" in Thorton Wilder's Pulitzer Prize-winning play *Our Town*. (The same role I played brilliantly at age 15 in Westminster High School's 1965 production.) Craven was also a writer, and among other credits, wrote the story for Laurel & Hardy's *Sons of the Desert*, one of the greatest movies of all time. (Well, in my opinion.)

Kay Caldwell is played as a Southern belle with the spiffy cultured vocal tones of Mayfair by the blonde actress Louise Allbritton, in a black wig. Kay's sister, Claire, the sunny heroine, is played by the blonde actress and beloved screen queen Evelyn Ankers, who isn't forced to wear a wig. It's not a cowboy movie, therefore the women can't wear black and white hats as signifiers, so the good sister has blonde hair and the sister in league with Dracula has black hair.

Professor Lazlo, a Hungarian Van Helsing, is played, in an astonishing example of appropriate casting, by an actual Hungarian, J. Edward Bromberg, a character actor best remembered for his comic rogues and villains, such as the evil governor of California oppressing Tyrone Power in *The Mark of Zorro*. Bromberg's authentic Hungarian accent helps to highlight Chaney's ear-eluding Hungarian dialect as "Count Alucard of Budapest."

Musical leading man Robert Paige gives an excellent performance as Frank, whose sanity grows increasingly frayed as the film progresses, achieving peace only in the final scene, as he watches the woman he loves burn.

In the minuscule role (one scene, in fact, only one sustained shot, and just a handful of lines) of the justice of the peace who performs Alucard and Kay's wedding is Robert Dudley. Dudley is well remembered and beloved as the "Weenie King" in Preston Sturges' comedy classic *The Palm Beach Story*. Though not given the kind of wonderful comedy material he had as the Weenie King, he manages to be amusing by the subtle glances he keeps giving Count Alucard, who clearly creeps him the hell out.

What's Good About It

Quite a lot. Robert Siodmak gave *Son of Dracula* a wonderful creamy-gothic look, while Curt based his story on an up-until-then overlooked idea, that to some people vampirism has extremely attractive attributes.

Robert Siodmak is quoted on the *Son of Dracula* DVD as saying:

> With so little actual horror in my own life, I'm essentially a mild-mannered, gentle fellow, who feels genuinely sorry for the condemned souls characterized in movies like *Son of Dracula*.

It's nice that he didn't let that Nazi Holocaust thing which he fled Europe to survive get him down.

The best-remembered gimmick in the film is Dracula's silly alias, "Alucard." Everyone over the age of 10 figures out that it is "Dracula" spelt in reverse long before the characters in the movie do, but that's probably intentional.

In one eerie, effective scene, Kay stops at a sewer. Alucard's coffin bobs to the surface. It seems Alucard snoozes his days away beneath stagnant sewage, on a layer of his native mud. A mist rises out of the coffin and solidifies into Alucard standing on his coffin, which he then sewage-surfs to shore.

In another good scene, as Lazlo describes how a vampire can slip into a room as a vapor and listen to his enemies plot against him, Alucard slips into the room as a vapor and listens to them plot against him.

Lazlo figures out Kay's plan to become a vampire deliberately, and says that she suffers from "thanatophobia, fear of death." Do you know anyone who *doesn't* have thanatophobia? Isn't that about as common as breathing?

Kay is a piece of work, inviting Dracula to her home, feeding her father to him, marrying him, and then asking her boyfriend to kill him. One wonders if she's also taken out life insurance on Alucard from Fred MacMurray. If James M. Cain had ever written a gothic, Kay Caldwell would have strutted in on long legs displayed by a slit up the side of her form-fitting shroud.

The climax, played without dialogue, is eerie and downbeat. The vampires are all dead, but the hero is going to jail for murder, and while sweet Claire now has the plantation and the money, her family is wiped out, and she never does have a boyfriend. Hmm. Hold that thought.

What's Bad About It

Lon Chaney Jr. Lon was not an untalented actor, but he is not suited to play any member of the Dracula family. The great actor Peter Lorre used to speak of two types of acting: acting from within and what he called "making faces." Chaney makes some really *intense faces* at us throughout this film.

Lon here is fat-cheeked and suavely mustachioed, with sharp little painted eyebrows that Divine would have killed for. He's built like a defensive linebacker, and he speaks with the voice of, well, Larry Talbot. He tries hard, but he can not rise above his miscasting. He can do menacing, but sinister is beyond his range, and suave is just plain impossible.

Dark Oaks is the creepiest, most moss-bedecked, decaying gothic plantation in the whole of the southern San Fernando Valley, Hell's Tara, surrounded by a sinister bayou. Yet no one, I repeat, *no one at all in the entire cast*, speaks with a Southern accent. Of course, the director was a German Jew with a poor command of English. Perhaps he heard nothing unusual in having a Southern plantation inhabited by what sounds like the population of Los Angeles, visited by a Transylvanian vampire who sounds like he was from Oklahoma.

Dr. Brewster is a no-nonsense, pragmatic, hang-the-red-tape-and-rules-just-get-the-job-done type that has made

America what it is today, with the medical ethics of Dr. Mengele. He strenuously suggests declaring Kay insane, even though he knows she is not, because, "We've got to protect Kay from herself." Who is going to protect her from Dr. Brewster? He's supposed to be *a good guy!* This movie was made in 1943, while we were supposed to be *fighting* fascists, not admiring them as folksy small-town doctors.

Later, Lazlo suggests Brewster get Claire to order the immediate cremation of Kay's body, before she can rise from her coffin, without telling Claire that her sister isn't quite dead. Is the doc horrified at this suggestion? Is he reluctant to burn semi-alive a woman he's known since the day he delivered her? Is he hesitant to trick Claire into ordering her sister burnt? No.

What's Gay About It

It's certainly less gay, at least on the surface, than *Dracula's Daughter*, but if we continue the basic metaphor of vampire attacks as sex, we find the theme still raging.

Alucard's first victim is his soon-to-be father-in-law. The hickeys on the colonel's throat alert Kay that her lover has not only humiliated her by standing her up in front of everyone she knows at the big ball in his honor, but that he has instead had sex with her own father, not to mention killing him. What a bad boyfriend for a cheating affianced woman.

Lazlo and Dr. Brewster, two middle-aged confirmed bachelors, room together. At one point, the doc confesses his heartbreaking realization about his unrequited love for the sheriff as well: "He's not quite ready to hold me." When Dr. Brewster finds himself alone with a deranged and vulnerable Frank, the good doctor then does just what you'd want your doctor to do: he slips Frank a rufie and lays him out on his consulting couch. We fade out before we can see what Brewster the Rooster does next.

Frank has already had a bad night. Not only has he killed his fiancée, but once Kay lay near death on the floor, Frank ran outside for a pretty good eerie dash through the swampy night, pursued by a large bat, ending, as do we all, in a graveyard.

Frank collapsed, and the bat landed on his *back* to bite, which amounts to Alucard spending his wedding night raping his bride's ex-fiance, with chasers of bestiality and necrophilia.

When Lazlo describes how vampires get blood by sucking their victim's throats, Brewster says, "That's a nauseating thought." Well, sure. He's looking at Lazlo's fat neck at the time, nor is Brewster's throat at all appetizing, but there are other, more suck-worthy esophagi around.

At another point, a woman enters Brewster's office bearing a young boy who's just been bitten. The mother's account that the boy said something about a foreign man in a fog tells us that Alucard is now molesting young boys. I'd have assumed Kay did it if it weren't for that "foreign man in a fog" line. The film makers go out of their way to make sure we know it was a gay pedophile attack. "Dracula's first victim," says Lazlo, who hasn't been paying much attention, since this is at least his fourth.

When the whole monstrousness of Kay's plan is revealed to him, Frank asks, "Do you expect me to agree to anything so fantastic?" Kay tells him he has no choice. She's taken the first step while he slept. "Frank," she purrs seductively, getting to the crux of the argument, "isn't eternity together better than a few years of ordinary life?" About this time, Frank should be seriously rethinking his heterosexuality, because this bitch has gotten his ass into some *deep* trouble.

And then there's Claire, the "good girl." Claire has no love interest, despite being a very beautiful, reasonably intelligent, non-obnoxious, and non-evil woman who is rolling in cash. Just why is she without a boy friend? Claire gets the plantation in the end, and all the family fortune, including whatever wealth Alucard may have brought along. She won't be getting Frank, but then, she's shown no interest in him or in any other male.

A paranoid theory: everything except Frank burning her up was Kay's master plan. Then that last gambit, based on an ethical trait in Frank that Kay, seduced as she was by the Dark Side of the Force, could neither understand nor foresee, swings the pendulum of fortune back Claire's way. (Frank setting fire to his only-somewhat-dead fiancée after killing her husband is not what is normally considered "ethical," but we can make an exception when the victims are undead monsters feeding on the living.)

Could it be that Claire wasn't Kay's sister for free? Could this actually be Claire's grand scheme; to let Kay founder in her own evil, morbid machinations, and then live happily ever after on the spoils? The spirit of James M. Cain does seem to be hanging about. It's almost *The Vampire Always Bites Twice* or *Double Undead-ity*. For straight men, this movie has only one conceivable message: watch out for women. They're bad news. How gay is that?

Aftermath

Though technically a sequel to *Dracula*, this movie is of a one-off. Dracula himself would return in three more Universal films, two of which we can dispose of quickly. The third we will hold for last.

6

HOUSE PARTIES
House of Frankenstein (1944)
House of Dracula (1945)

(Just the Dracula bits)

I see glimpses of a strange world...
— Rita Hussman (Anne Gwynne), making the most of her only good scene, in *House of Frankenstein*

In 1943, Universal crammed two of their monsters into one movie in *Frankenstein Meets the Wolfman*. It made a lot of money, so Curt Siodmak was charged with concocting a story that would include Frankenstein's Monster, Larry Talbot, Count Dracula, a mad scientist, and a hunchbacked assistant. He knocked out something titled *The Devil's Brood* and then lit out of Universal. Curt seldom discussed the movie and claimed never to have seen it.

Since the films would feature Dracula himself again, this would be a good opportunity to return Bela Lugosi to the role, right? He had played Dracula in all-but-name in MGM's *Mark of the Vampire* and in Columbia's *Return of the Vampire*, a movie constructed like a sequel to a movie that had never been made. Lon was busy playing Larry Talbot. Lugosi was available.

But Universal cast John Carradine. Carradine was a fine actor, with a justly famous, booming, sinister voice, who was an habitual breeder, with more sons than Frankenstein and Dracula put together. His Count Dracula is dapper, suave, sinister, seductive, and distinctly American. It's a critical darling of a performance, often cited as the best of Universal's Count Draculas. It *is* a good performance. As a vampire from Albany, he'd be spiffy, but he certainly didn't sound like he'd spent much time in Romania. He doesn't even attempt an accent.

Somewhere in a Europe were World War II is not raging, mad, menacing, and vicious Dr. Gustav Niemann (Boris Karloff) and his longtime companion/hunchbacked assistant/sinister sidekick Daniel (J. Carrol Naish) escape from prison and steal a traveling chamber of horrors, the central exhibit of which is a skeleton in a coffin with a stake stuck through its ribs, billed as the actual skeleton of Count Dracula, who is now, evidently, as famous and feared as Donald Trump. For some reason, people think it's a fake.

It's not, since, when Karloff pulls the out the stake from the skeleton's rib cage, Dracula's body reforms on the skeleton, layer by layer, from bones to veins to organs to nerves to skin to *clothes*, until he's fully reconstituted, in his usual full formal dress, replete with cape. Idiotic, but just as well. Do you really want to see John Carradine naked?

Gustav and Dracula make a deal. If Dracula will kill an old enemy of his, Gustav will keep Dracula's coffin safe for him. So Dr. Gustav Niemann thinks *Count Dracula* is a reliable ally. Does that seem like a good idea to you? Spoiler alert: it's not.

Since Dracula is now famous, Dracula produces another alias. This time he's Baron Latos from Transylvania. This is a considerable improvement over "Count Alucard" (and over "Count DeVille," an unsubtle alias Dracula uses in the novel), although I wonder why he kept the "from Transylvania" part. He sounds more like he's from Pennsylvania than Transylvania.

Karloff's enemy is "Old Hussmann" (Sig Rumann on loan from the Marx Brothers movies), who is strolling home from the chamber of horrors with his grandson, "Young Hussmann," aka Carl (dreamy Peter Coe) and Carl's American bride Rita (lovely Ann Gwynne, who happens to be the grandmother of Chris Pine, our latest Captain Kirk), when Dracula gallops up in a private coach. Where the hell did Dracula get a coach and driver? Gustav pulled the stake out of Dracula just as Hussmann left the exhibit, and he's still on his way home, so it's just a few minutes later, and Dracula has acquired a coach and driver. Did Dracula have a fairy godmother and a pumpkin? Dracula invites everyone to join him in a glass of wine, although I have it from a very reliable source that he never touches the stuff.

Carl can't wait to leave his new bride alone with Baron Latos, who is a suave smoothy. Using hypnosis, Dracula shows Rita "a strange world of people who are dead and yet alive." Sounds like West Hollywood at 3am to me. Rita becomes Dracula's slave, like you do, without losing so much as a drop of blood. Dracula arranges to elope with her later that night. He moves fast, but then, he has to. The interval from his revival to his destruction in this movie is only fourteen minutes.

Dracula then confronts his assigned victim, Old Hussmann. Carradine and Sig Rumann make intense faces at each other, and then we see Dracula turn into a bat via wall shadows. The bat's shadow lands on Hussmann's shadow to drink his blood's shadow.

Dracula then kidnaps Rita, since he hasn't had a busy enough night. While Dracula and Rita escape in Dracula's coach, Carl finds his dead grandfather, and immediately phones Inspector Arnz, played by series stand-by Lionel Atwill, although if members of my family were falling prey to a vampire, I don't think Lionel Atwill would be my first call.

The chase is on. Gustav, seeing the cops coming, assumes they're after him from force of habit. Now it's Gustav, Daniel, and the show wagons in front, Dracula and Rita in second place, and Carl, Arnz, and the police on horseback bringing up the rear, all thundering across locations in the Santa Monica mountains above Malibu, near where *M*A*S*H* was shot.

Just where does Dracula think he's going? Sunrise is coming quite soon. His coffin is in Gustav's wagon. He hasn't a chance of catching up with Carl and the cops hot on his trail. He should just abandon Rita, transform into a bat, fly over to Gustav's wagon and sack out.

He doesn't.

Gustav decides it's time to cut the shroud strings. In a nice bit of stunt work for an otherwise cheap film, J. Carroll Naish's hunch-stunt-double runs back over the roofs of the two wagons and dumps Dracula's coffin out the back door. The pin holding Dracula's horses to the coach comes flying out for no reason other than to add some arbitrary additional action. Carradine's stunt double leaps from the coach, which rolls over down an embankment.

Dracula makes a run for it, but he's too late. The rising sun catches him. He, *and his clothes,* fade away, and all that's left is that skeleton again. Fortunately, Rita is unharmed after rolling down a hill in a tumbling vehicle with no seat belts nor roll bar, apparently being made of Silly Putty. She comes out of her trance in her husband's arms, and they're happy together, with her never even having been bitten. Of course, Old Hussmann is dead, but time heals everything, and that was over five minutes ago, so they've moved on, as has the movie. Cheek to cherubic cheek, they gaze into an untroubled future, while Gustav and Daniel ride on to the next segment of the film, which we will look at later.

The standard conventional wisdom on Universal's monster rally movies at the time of *House of Dracula* is that the characters were played out. This is absurd. Many another film-maker in the years since has shown there were plenty of ways still to go with Dracula, Frankenstein, and werewolves and such.

But there *was* something played out all right; the extremely limited imaginations of the creative minds behind these films. Even Curt Siodmak, whose imagination was not limited, was out of ideas for them, so he left Universal.

That these movies are so bereft of ideas, intelligence, or freshness is not the characters' faults. All they needed was someone with fresh ideas, and some executives who wouldn't say, "No, that's different from what we did before." What was played out was doing the *same* stories over and over, with minute variations, because the front office is afraid of originality. It's the sort of "thinking" that will always prefer doing a sequel to or a remake of a previously successful film rather than doing something new.

Sadly for the monsters, *House of Frankenstein* made a lively profit, so *House of Dracula* was inevitable. The same team, and some of the same cast, were rounded back up. Unfortunately, this did not include Boris Karloff, who had fled to RKO, where he and Val Lewton were having the temerity to make *good* movies.

"Dr. Edelmann's Creature Clinic" would have made more sense as a title for *House of Dracula*, because in this film, all the monsters come to Dr. Edelmann (Onslow Stevens) to be cured of being monsters. Sound familiar? Yes, Dr. Edelmann is running one of those clinics that promises to "cure" movie homosexuality. We never go anywhere near Castle Dracula or Carfax Abbey.

Dracula, John Carradine once again, arrives first, asking to be cured of his vampirism. Okay, now Dracula's vampirism is a supernatural curse, laid on him by Satan in return for military victories a few centuries back. Why would he seek a medical cure for a supernatural curse? Does he think Franz Edelmann is more powerful than the king of Hell? And given that being "cured" of his vampirism would mean his death, why does he want to be cured? If he just wants to be free of it all, why not just go sunbathe?

Come to think of it, what is he doing here at all? He and his clothes died in the previous movie, yet here he and his wardrobe are, alive and spiffy again, with no explanation. Did someone ask the children of Visaria to clap if they believed in vampires?

There's another lure for Dracula at Edelmann's clinic, Edelmann's assistant, Miliza Morelle, played by Martha O'Driscoll.

Franz believes he's found a "parasite" in Dracula's blood that may be the reason he's lived for four hundred years (can I have some of that parasite, please?) and can change his species at will. That's one hell of a parasite. Franz proposes a course of transfusions, or as Dracula usually calls them, snacks.

Dr. Edelmann is such a noble doctor that he transfuses his own blood into Dracula. I've had transfusions myself, but my doctor always used *other* people's blood, the selfish bastard! Need I add that, given my dictum that sharing blood with a vampire equals sex, Dracula has now begun an affair with Dr. Edelmann. I just hope he doesn't break Franz's heart.

Dracula finds Miliza playing Beethoven's *Moonlight Sonata* on the piano. Dracula makes a face at Miliza while she plays, and she begins improvising new stuff, which Dracula declares to be beautiful, although it is no improvement on Beethoven to my tin ears. He says, "It's the music of the world from which I come." (It's from the Universal Music Department? Oh, right.

It is.) The scene obviously is lifted right out of the screenplay from *Dracula's Daughter*.

The music, and Dracula's face, both grow more intense, until Miliza's hand wanders to the crucifix around her neck, which makes Dracula turn away, and restores Beethoven to the piano. I've known several professional pianists, and they seldom have a hand free to finger jewelry when playing a piano, but Miliza can play *Moonlight Sonata* with one hand. What dexterity!

It finally dawns on Franz that exposing his employees, which includes a female hunchbacked assistant named Nina, to Dracula's presence was perhaps a tad irresponsible.

Franz interrupts Drac's tryst with Miliza just as he'd gotten her to toss her cross away. Franz tells Drac he needs another transfusion, right now.

During the transfusion, Dracula uses his power of making faces to put Franz into a trance, reverses the transfusion, and deliberately gives Franz some of his tainted blood. He has no particular reason to do this. It's pure maliciousness. While I prefer characters to have motivations for their actions, I guess I can accept pure maliciousness from Count Dracula.

Franz wakes up once Dracula leaves the room, and heads upstairs to save Miliza. Franz brandishes a large crucifix, which sends Dracula scurrying off, while Miliza faints into the arms of Larry "The Wolfman" Talbot, part of a growing romantic relationship between them in another plot line.

Fleeing from Franz, Dracula runs to the basement. Dawn arrives seconds after he closes his coffin lid, for which he should thank Edelmann—if he'd tarried longer with Miliza, he'd never have made it. But then Dr. Edelmann, like all his medical predecessors in these movies, tosses his "first do no harm" oath out the window, in this case, the window allowing the sun to shine into the basement, so that when Franz drags Dracula's coffin below it and pulls back the lid, Dracula and his clothes die and fade away.

Franz says, "The evil that I brought here will never live again," but Dracula has an appointment three years on with a couple of mugs named Abbott & Costello. At Universal, you can't keep a bad man down.

There were a few other vampire movies of the 1930s and 1940s, including Lugosi's *Mark of the Vampire* at MGM and *Return of the Vampire* at Columbia, both mentioned earlier, and there was a terrible movie with Lionel Atwill, Fay Wray, and Dwight Frye called *The Vampire Bat*. However, both *Mark of the Vampire* and *The Vampire Bat* are cheats, as their vampires turn out to be fakes.

The relatively obscure *Return of the Vampire*, with Lugosi as a bloodsucker named Armond Tesla because Universal owned the rights to Count Dracula, was a fairly offbeat picture which, unlike Universal's 1940s horror movies, actually noticed that World War II was going on, and used the London Blitz in the plot. Tesla has a sinister sidekick who is a werewolf, so the movie wasn't free of the tendency to mash monsters together. But *Return of the Vampire* was a one-off anomaly, Columbia trying to turn a buck off Universal's fan base, and is largely forgotten today except for loyal Bela Lugosi and Nina Foch fans.

WHAT'S IN A NAME?

Dracula is a really cool sounding evil name, but what does it mean? "Frankenstein" is easy to translate. It means "Frank's Beer Mug." Not scary. Anyway, "Dracula" means "Son of Dracul" or "Little Dracul" or "Dracul Jr," like "Lon Chaney Jr." Vlad Dracula's father was called Dracul, so *Son of Dracula* could reasonably have been titled *Draculala*.

But what does "Dracul" mean? Well, it means "devil" or "dragon," so "Dracula" means "Son of the Devil" or "Little Dragon," or "Satan Jr." Now that is an evil-sounding name. Remember all those times your mom called you a little devil? Well, she was saying you are Dracula!

7

DIE, MUMMY, DIE!
The Mummy (1932)

I loved you once, but now you belong with the dead.
— Princess Anck-es-en-Amon aka Helen Grosvenor (Zita Johann) being ageist in *The Mummy*.

There is a saying: "Life begins at 40." In gay life, the saying is precisely the reverse. That this quote is spoken by Helen Grosvenor, aka Princess Anck-es-en-Amon (or maybe it's the other way around) to Ardath Bey, aka Imhoptep, in Universal's 1932 *The Mummy* tells you why, as the years have rolled past, that my admiration for this superb film has only grown greater.

The Story

A pair of British archaeologists unearth the mummy of an ancient priest, 3700-year-old Imhotep, as well as the Scroll of Thoth, which every school kid knows was used by Isis to raise Osiris from the dead. When one of the scientists reads the scroll aloud, Imhotep wakes up, steals the scroll, and wanders off into the night, to the never-ending amusement of the scientist, who literally dies laughing.

Eleven years later, Imhotep, now calling himself Ardath Bey, leads another team of British archaeologists to the unplundered tomb of Princess Anck-es-en-Amon so they can plunder it. Anck-es-en-Amon was Imhotep's forbidden girlfriend back in ancient Egypt, and Ardath intends to restore her to life as he was restored. But her soul has been reincarnated as Helen Grosvenor. (We never learn why Imhotep was never reincarnated. Punishment for Blasphemy? No one ever wanted to be him?) Ardath Bey tries to kill Helen, so she can be resurrected as a living mummy like himself (every girl's dream), telling her she must "face moments of horror for an eternity of love," neatly describing many a wedding night. The princess's repentant prayers to Isis prompts the goddess to intervene, divinely killing Imhotep and reducing his body to dust. The Scroll of Thoth burns.

The Production

In the wake of *Frankenstein*'s enormous success, Boris Karloff was a huge star. A year before he was playing tiny roles, such as in 1931's *The Mad Genius* (where he wasn't even the titular mad genius, the role essayed by the great John Barrymore), or his "First Revolutionary" in the nearly forgotten comedy team of Wheeler & Woolsey's *Cracked Nuts* (which is, by the way, a very funny movie), or playing the heavy in not-at-all-forgotten comedy team Laurel & Hardy's prison comedy *Pardon Us*, but in the French language version only. (The French *Pardon Us* is now a lost film, so you can't even see him with Laurel & Hardy except in stills.) Boris was lucky even to get billing in most of his pre-1932 movies; he barely got billed in *Frankenstein*. But in 1932, after *Frankenstein* had turned into a mega-hit, as "Karloff," or even "Karloff the Uncanny," he began being billed above the title in thrillers like *The Old Dark House*, *The Mask of Fu Manchu*, and *The Mummy*.

Karloff's billing in *The Old Dark House* (a perfectly wonderful black comedy, sort of an early run at the Addams Family) belied that it was a non-speaking supporting role, far less prominent in the movie than the lower-billed "supporting cast" which included Gloria Stuart, Charles Laughton, Melvin Douglas, and Raymond Massey, not to mention the lesser-known Ernest Thesiger, who stole the movie from all of them. *Mask of Fu Manchu* (a wildly racist romp with Karloff camping it up in racial make-up, clearly having too much fun) was at MGM.

Universal needed a vehicle for their new star, Karloff. (After one movie, *Murders in the Rue Morgue*, Universal was so over Bela Lugosi.) The brouhaha about the supposed Curse of King Tut's Tomb inspired Carl Laemmle Jr. to retool a treatment for a film on Cagliostro, a famous dead (or *is* he?) magician later played by Orson Welles, into an Egyptian-themed Karloff film.

SHE WHO MUST BE HILARIOUS

Universal never made *SHE*, but RKO, Merian C. Cooper, and *Dracula's Daughter*'s Irving Pichel did in 1935, and it is the silliest, campiest movie you've ever laid eyes on, and if you haven't laid eyes on it, rent it or buy it. You won't believe it. In *SHE*, they reduced the age of She Who Must Be Obeyed from 3000 in the novel to a more youthful 500, because they didn't want the movie to seem *ridiculous*. (And allow me to recommend the H. Rider Haggard novel as well. It's gloriously over-the-top insane, and much sexier than any of the movie versions. Queen Ayesha seldom bothers wearing clothes, even when holding court, and she uses the dried-out corpses of the past citizens of the Lost City of Kor as torches to illuminate nighttime events.)

RKO also replaced the African jungle setting of the novel's Lost City of Kor with an even more bizarre, art deco lost city *under a glacier in the Arctic*!

The movie is sublime nonsense disguised as an adventure fantasy. It's available on DVD and Blu-ray in a colorized version (though it's a movie that is impossible to vandalize, no matter how hard you try), and with a commentary track from Ray Harryhausen, who loved the movie but utterly failed to see the camp, and takes it un-ironically as a serious adventure story. *Tarzan of the Apes* is a more believable adventure story. Well, Ray also considered *King Kong* a deep, stark human drama.

Screenwriter for *The Mummy* John Balderston was simultaneously crafting an adaptation of H. Rider Haggard's campy fantasy adventure *SHE!* In constructing a story for what became *The Mummy*, he felt no compunction about swiping Haggard's story and reversing the genders of the two main characters.

SHE! is the story of a 3000-year-old African queen who meets the reincarnation of her ancient boyfriend, and tries to lure him into unnatural eternal life and love with her, but who ends up having all her years catch up with her at once.

The Mummy is the story of a 3700-year-old Egyptian high priest who meets the reincarnation of his ancient girlfriend, and tries to lure her into unnatural eternal life and love with him, but who ends up having all his years catch up with him at once. Just to show he was an equal-opportunity plagiarist, Balderston also freely helped himself to his *own* screen adaptation of *Dracula*, turning *The Mummy* into a virtual remake of that earlier hit. This was reinforced by Universal casting Edward Van Sloan and David Manners in roles *identical* to their *Dracula* characters, though they did have to learn new character names.

Karloff's Imhotep, like Dracula, is an ancient aristocrat whose life has been unnaturally prolonged, who has hypnotic powers, who stalks David Manners' girlfriend, placing her under his hypnotic influence to make her over into the same sort of unnatural thing he is, and who is opposed by Edward Van Sloan's pompous professorial authority on all things supernatural.

Karl Freund, the 360-pound genius cinematographer who had shot *The Golem*, *Metropolis*, *All Quiet on the Western Front*, and *Dracula*, was given the assignment of making his directorial debut with *The Mummy*. Freund's camera keeps *The Mummy* from ever lapsing into boredom.

The day they shot the scene in which Imhotep awakens from the dead was a miserable day for Boris. He had spent eight hours having Jack Pierce apply his make-up and the bandages. Every account of the film emphasizes this ordeal, as though Karloff spent every day of the shoot enduring eight hours in make-up. Actually, he wore this extreme make-up, which looks great though it bears scant resemblance to an actual mummy, on only a single shooting day. The rest of the time he wore the far less arduous and time-consuming Ardath Bey make-up.

THE UNTOLD TALE OF IMHOTEP

At the beginning of *The Mummy*, Imhotep arises from the dead, steals the Scroll of Thoth, and shuffles off into the night, where the archaeologists quickly lose all trace of him. This is beyond belief, even for a movie whose lead character is 3700 years old. He's shuffling along at about one mile an hour, he leaves a trail of rotting bandages and mold, and it's not like a walking mummy wouldn't stand out in a crowd, no matter how poor and ragged the other people in the crowd might be. Also, it's his first time outside in 3700 years. He doesn't know where he is or where he's going. He just goes.

We next see him in his identity of Ardath Bey, ten years later. He now has money, a house, and a perfect command of English, with even a slight British accent. The movie gives no hint whatever about Imhotep's missing ten years.

That's the story I'd like to see. What was it like to wake up after three millennia, in a world utterly unlike the world you left, not knowing a living human being nor a word of any living language? What do you do? Where do you go? How did Ardath spend that decade? How did he learn English? What other languages did he learn? How much of the intervening history of earth has he learned? How did he acquire his capital?

We'll never learn that part of the story, but it tantalizes me.

What's Good About It

Almost everything. Beautifully directed and shot by Freund, well-acted by Zita Johnann and Karloff, almost devoid of any humor or comic relief, and using lighting and mood more than shock and violence to achieve its effects, *The Mummy* rises above its absurdities to remain a potent chiller that reminds us that, after forty, give it up. Unnatural sex is only for the young.

Karloff's performance resembles Lugosi's as Dracula. He is usually extremely still, speaks slowly, and has glowing eyes. (Freund had tried this "glowing eyes" effect unsuccessfully in *Dracula*, often resulting in Dracula having one glowing eye and one glowing cheek. In *The Mummy*, he got it so it works every time.) But where Lugosi was stiff and often a bit dull, Karloff is riveting. Boris had the advantage of acting in his native language, so he knew how to pronounce the words and where to inflect. Additionally, Karloff understood and embraced the concept of underplaying.

Karloff's Ardath Bey looks great for a man his age. Tall, whip-thin, befezzed like the world's most-sinister Shriner, jet-black eyebrows, skin admittedly in serious need of some moisturizer, and speaking perfect English, Karloff kept all movement to the barest minimum, and avoids all physical contact. His stillness commands the screen. And his resemblance to an erection is hard to miss and completely intentional. (Ardath Bey is an undead sex symbol, basically a necrophilia symbol.)

Helen and Anck-es-en-Amon are played by the exotic Hungarian actress Zita Johann, a flat-chested knockout of a beauty. A Broadway actress and an anti-Hollywood snob, Zita left California in a huff after making this movie, leaving a small film legacy. (She has only eight film credits on the IMDb.) Her later interviews reveal a woman who was theatrical to the point of extreme affectation. Next to her, Norma Desmond was a down-home farm girl. She was also a bit of a new-age loon, the Shirley MacLaine of her day, only not possessing an ear-splittingly shrill voice like Shirl's.

According to her interviews, Freund chose her to be his scapegoat, in case the movie tanked, and she said he treated her abominably throughout the shoot. I emphasize that this is her version of events. If true, then karma found its revenge, since Freund would go on to be the director of photography on *I Love Lucy*, inventing the multi-camera lighting and photography techniques still in common use on television today. Years of working with the iron-willed, abrasive Lucille Ball would expiate any sins against actresses Freund that may have accrued.

The shots of Karloff being wrapped up in his mummy bandages while still alive and struggling are truly horrifying and can still creep you out today.

What's Bad About It

We are again treated to Edward Van Sloan's ponderous pompousness, and to David Manners' effeminate version of a macho hero. We are told Van Sloan's Dr. Muller is a master of "occult sciences." What exactly are they? An occult scientist is rather like a deaf singer. Dr. Muller has never met an ancient superstition he doesn't believe in as literal truth. Muller would never fall for rationalist poppycock like global warming or evolution.

Manners' Frank Whemple is a remarkably dim bulb for a scientist, with a lightening-quick grasp of the bleeding obvious. At one point Frank says, "Queer story that young Oxford chap going mad. You know what I think it was?"

"No, what?" asks fellow archaeologist and straight man Dr. Pearson.

"I think he went crazy."

When coming on to Helen *in Cairo*, Frank says, "You know, I'd have liked Egypt better if I'd met you there." Where does he think Cairo is? Just outside Pittsburgh? Frank prattles on about opening Anck-es-en-Amon's tomb, and even says that, looking at the mummy princess' withered, dead face, "You'd think me silly, but I sort of fell in love with her."

"Silly" isn't the word that springs into Helen's mind, nor into mine. "Do you have to open graves to find girls to fall in love with?" Helen asks, making explicit the creepy undercurrent of necrophilia on which this whole film hinges. Oh, and the answer to Helen's question about Frank having to dig up dates is, "Yes." Any living woman's gaydar would have warned her off of Frank instantly.

A NOBLE JOHNSON

The Whemple's Nubian servant (essentially the same role as Joan Standing's "Briggs," in the *Mummy*-as-*Dracula*-remake perspective on the movie) was played by Noble Johnson (a name that sounds like what a very-full-of-himself man might call his primary reproductive organ), a black actor best remembered as the zombie who sadly fails to kill Bob Hope in *The Ghost Breakers*, and as the native chiefs in Merian C. Cooper's *King Kong, Son of Kong*, and *SHE*. This was the man who popularized that beloved 1930's catch phrase, "*Ana Saba Kong!*" which Ray Bradbury or Peter Jackson could tell you means "Bride of Kong."

A friend since boyhood of Lon Chaney, along with being a large, well-built mass of muscular character actor who, among other roles, had played Queequeg to John Barrymore's Captain Ahab in the first sound film of *Moby Dick* (though it's doubtful Melville would have recognized his masterful novel in that silly-but-enjoyable movie), Noble Johnson was also the first black movie mogul, who founded and ran, from 1916 to 1921, the all-black Lincoln Motion Picture Company, the first studio exclusively making films about the black experience, portraying black people as genuine, three-dimensional persons, and not just the caricatures and stereotypes they were limited to portraying at the major studios. He was a skilled actor and a man who lived up to his name. He lived to be 96.

Helen tries shutting him down by saying, "Don't you think I've had enough excitement for one evening without the additional thrill of a strange man making love to me?" I've always been in favor of that additional thrill myself, but I'll grant her that Frank is certainly a strange man. For instance, later in the picture, Frank would sound like a love-happy teenage boy as he asks, "Do you think I have a chance [with Helen]?" if he wasn't saying it with his father's fresh corpse *literally lying at his feet!* Frank manages, via deft footwork, not to stumble over his dad's cadaver as he dashes off to call Helen and make a date.

In a celebrated sequence, Ardath uses his magic pool to show Helen a lot of exposition from the last 3700 years, including a remarkably gory for 1932 scene of the slaves who buried her being impaled on spears. "You will not remember what I show you now," Ardath says, making the whole scene pointless.

What's Gay About It

Here we have the quintessential older gay man love story, the tale of a man who only wants to reunite with the great love of his life, yet who is cruelly rejected merely because he's a tad over forty. Okay, he's around 3740, and, of course, technically he's dead. True, that "great love" is presented as a woman, but we all know that straight women find men over forty distinguished. It is gay men who think that after forty you're only fit for embalming.

In the very first scene, Bramwell Fletcher who, though heterosexual in real life (he was married then to *Dracula*'s bloodless Helen Chandler), was nonetheless every bit as virility-challenged as David Manners onscreen, playing the soon-to-go-mad young archaeologist who accidentally revives Imhotep, calls the mummy a "very peculiar gentleman." He should talk. When asked why the mummy was subjected to his hideous fate, Fletcher's minced conjecture is, "Maybe he got too gay with the vestal virgins." As it happens, he's partially correct.

At first, Ardath spends time in the Cairo Museum, mooning over the mummy of his late girlfriend who, like many wealthy women, is totally wrapped up in herself. But once Ardath gets a gander at Helen, a version of Anck-es-en-Amon who isn't a dried-up 3700-year-old corpse, well, let's just say he pitches a tent in the desert. Seldom has romantic obsession been played as blatantly as in this scene. Ardath never takes his burning eyes off of Helen for a second, nor does she avert her stare from his wrinkly kisser. He knows now that Anckes-en-Amon's soul is in Helen's far more desirable form. What a stroke of luck.

There's a scene where a Nubian servant, played by Nobel Johnson, admits Ardath into the house. Ardath's eyes light up, literally, at the sight of the tall, hunky black man, and Ardath mumbles some inaudible words, which cause Nobel instantly to kneel before the older man.

The surprisingly lavish flashback to ancient Egypt sequence is full of hot black men in short skirts and little else, and they all get speared, unfortunately with actual spears.

In the film's climax, the princess has an attack of ageism greater than a twenty-one-year-old circuit queen at an over-forty mixer. "No! I'm alive! I'm young! I won't die. I loved you once, but now you belong with the dead." Whether she objects more to their 3700-year age difference or to his being dead isn't clear. What is clear is that his centuries of devotion doesn't mean squat as far as she's concerned. The young, they can be so shallow. One finally is amused to see her true hideous fate: marrying limp-wristed, passing-for-straight Frank.

Aftermath

Universal never made a sequel to *The Mummy*. The Laemmles realized they had a one-off. Besides, when the goddess Isis reduces your leading character to dust, even a Hollywood mogul can't bring him back. So when the Universal brass of 1940 decided to try mummy-making for money-making, they created a new mummy, if that's not a contradiction in terms, in four regrettably forgettable movies.

8

WHAT'S A MUMMY TO DO?: THE KHARIS MUMMY MOVIES

The Mummy's Hand (1940)
The Mummy's Tomb (1942)
The Mummy's Ghost (1944)
The Mummy's Curse (1944)

> *I swear by the mighty power of Amon-Ra, whose anger can shatter the world, that I will not betray my trust.*
> — Every high priest of Karnak/Arkam in all of these movies

The only even remotely watchable entry in the Kharis mummy series is the first, *The Mummy's Hand*, and it's terrible. The other three, *Tomb*, *Ghost*, and *Curse*, are so interchangeably awful that I have remained for fifty years unable to remember which title goes with which movie. When you give sequels titles like *Return of*, *Bride of*, *Son of*, and the *Prisoner of Azkaban*, and *Abbott & Costello Meets*, there's a clear order. (Roman numerals would, you'd think, make sequel order clear, but that was before the fourth, fifth, and sixth *Star Wars* movies were Roman numeraled *I*, *II*, and *III*.)

In *The Mummy's Hand*, Dick Foran (an actor with the misfortune to resemble Nelson Eddy, so not sexy at all) plays Steve Banning, a down-on-his-luck archaeologist, a bargain-basement Indiana Jones, who, with "Babe" Jenson, played by Wallace Ford of *Freaks* and Hitchcock's *Spellbound* and *Shadow of a Doubt*, find their own temple of doom, the Temple of Karnak in the Hill of the Seven Jackals, where a living mummy named Kharis guards the tomb of the Princess Ananka.

Eventually, a girl friend for Banning emerges in Marta Solvani, played by Peggy Moran, an actress whose career spanned the era 1939 to 1942 like a pontoon bridge, just barely afloat, and then sunk without a trace, apart from *The Mummy's Hand*. Also in the cast is George Zucco as the Evil High Priest of Karnak, Andoheb. (Apparently, in Karnakism, the office actually is "Evil High Priest.")

At the top of the movie there's a scene where the old, dying Evil High Priest passes the torch (in this case, *literally* a torch) to Andoheb. His sole job, it seems, is to brew a tea made of "tana leaves" to feed the living mummy Kharis, played by cowboy actor Tom Tyler, which enables Kharis to wreak the curse of Amon-Ra, whose anger, we are repeatedly told, can shatter the world (though it seldom achieves even the most modest goals), on unbelievers and/or infidels who would dare defile the tomb of Princess Ananka, Kharis' old girlfriend. Why didn't King Tut get a living mummy to guard his tomb, or Ramses or Cheops or Cleopatra? How does Ananka rate?

Jack Pierce put the time-consuming mummy make-up on Tyler only once, and all of Kharis' close-ups were then shot on that single day. For the rest of the movie, Tyler is wearing a mummy mask. In the movie's sole effective creepy touch, in all of Tyler's close-ups the mummy's eyes were hand-painted, frame-by-frame, a solid black.

The Mummy's Hand is slower moving than Kharis himself. To quote Addison DeWitt in *All About Eve*, the "minutes fly like hours." It takes them forever to get to the tomb and wake up Kharis. Andoheb then gets the bright notion to have Kharis kidnap Marta, since Banning is too taken with Babe to pay her much mind anyway, and then give both her and himself some tana tea and become immortal lovers. Babe shoots Andoheb, and Banning sets fire to Kharis, and everyone else lives happily ever after until the sequel.

The sequel, *The Mummy's Tomb*, came out two years later. Lon Chaney Jr. took over the role of Kharis, except when Kharis was being played by stuntman Eddie Parker, which was generally in all scenes shot after lunch. Lon was cast solely for his name value. In fact, this is the movie where he dropped the

"Jr" and became billed simply as his father. Well, his father was dead, and there's no life in this role, either.

Jack Pierce didn't even bother with make-up. Chaney wears a bandage suit and a one-eyed mask. Since he has no dialogue, there's simply no way to tell in any scene if it is Lon Chaney, Eddie Parker, or Harpo Marx. One might suspect that Chaney never actually worked a day on any of his three mummy movies if it wasn't for the fact that he never stopped grousing about how much he hated the thankless, uncomfortable role. Lon wasn't the stoic masochist his father had been.

The Mummy's Tomb is set thirty years after *The Mummy's Hand*, with Dick Foran and Wallace Ford made up to look like mummies themselves, which is more than Chaney is. Luckily for Peggy Moran, her character has died along with her career. Babe Jenson, realizing that he has an awfully effeminate name for a man, has changed it to Babe *Hanson*. Yes, much butcher. (I mean, it *must* be intentional, mustn't it? It can't be that no one at the studio, including the actor who had played the role in both movies, remembered what the character's name was, nor ever even bothered to look at the movie or the script of the movie they were making the sequel to. Because that would just be incompetent.)

The problem is, *The Mummy's Hand*, judging by the fashions, the cars, and the topical references, appears to take place in 1940, while *The Mummy's Tomb*, allegedly set 30 years later, appears to take place in 1942.

The new Evil High Priest of Karnak, Mehemet Bey, is played by the hyper-dreamy 1940s sex god Turhan Bey. To state it plainly, Turhan was hot. Bey was a Turkish-Czechoslovakian actor, born in Vienna with the enormous name Turhan Gilbert Selahattin Sahultavy.

Not-quite-dead-after-all Andoheb assigns Mehemet the task of taking Kharis to Mapleton, Massachusetts, to kill all the unbelievers who defiled the Tomb of Ananka. Being killed ten minutes before they die of old age, that'll teach those unbelievers.

One might wonder why Andoheb waited for thirty years to get around to doing this, since it was his only task at hand. Maybe he spent the intervening years over-feeding Kharis, who is considerably bulkier than he was thirty years before. Chaney's mummy has to be the only person ever to gain weight after he died.

Once in America, Mehemet Bey unleashes Kharis on a killing spree. Kharis kills Steve, Babe, and Steve's sister Jane, played by Mary Gordon, who was basically ever-present in Universal pictures of the 1930s and 1940s (Karloff's Frankenstein Monster kills her in *Bride of Frankenstein*), and is best known as Mrs. Hudson, Sherlock Holmes' landlady throughout the entire Rathbone-Bruce Holmes series.

The mummy movies have always been ageist, but this is a new low. All of Kharis' victims are senior citizens (though they're spring chickens next to Kharis). Of course, it is worth noting that any healthy young person could outrun the slowly shuffling mummy without breaking a sweat.

The sheriff and his mob of villagers do what any right-thinking bunch of homophobes would do under the circumstances: they shoot down Bey and then kill the mummy via the sensible, restrained tactic of burning down the Banning mansion with him in it, not that burning him up had proved effective in the last movie. I think audiences may have found that the sixty-minute *The Mummy's Tomb* ended before they'd finished their popcorn.

Two years later, Universal decided to resurrect Kharis yet again in *The Mummy's Ghost*. Since Mehemet Bey, Kharis, and all the infidels who defiled the Tomb of Ananka are dead (along with an old lady sister of a defiler), one sees little point to it, but the Kharis pictures were made so cheaply, you'd think ten paid admissions would put them in the black.

Ghost opens with basically the exact same scene both previous Kharis films opened with. Back in Egypt, still-not-completely-dead Andoheb recounts the backstory to his latest successor as Evil High Priest of Karnak, Yousef Bey, played by John Carradine this time, except the job is now Evil High Priest of Arkham. Well, you couldn't expect them to remember it was Karnak for an entire two years, now could you? That would require paying attention to the previous movies they were making a sequel to.

In Mapleton, Kharis has bounced back from his latest cremation on his own, and is wandering around the Mapleton woods, looking for infidels to kill, or at least a tana bush.

It turns out that local girl Amina Mansouri ("Amina Mansouri," "Marta Solvani," none of the heroines of these movies are ever named Nancy Smith) is the reincarnation of Princess Ananka. That's handy. It would have been terribly inconvenient if Ananka had reincarnated in a woman in Cairo or Paris or Reseda. Amina was played by Ramsey Ames, an actress best remembered as "Party Guest" in *Mildred Pierce*. I'm afraid she got typed as "Party Guest," as she subsequently played the same role in in *Too Young to Know* (Directed by Johnny Carson's longtime producer, Freddy De Cordova), which I'd never before suspected was a sequel to *Mildred Pierce*. She was, for some years, married to Dale Wasserman, the author of the magnificent musical *Man of LaMancha*.

Yousef decides his mission is now to reunite the long-sundered lovers Kharis and Ananka, though if Karnak or Arkham or whomever the pertinent god is had really wanted them reunited, he'd had 3000 years in which to accomplish it. Wasn't it their love being *forbidden* that launched this whole lame saga in the first place?

Amina's hair acquires white streaks, so that she looks like a cross between the Bride of Frankenstein and Cruella DeVil. Her boyfriend, Tom, played by Robert Lowry, never notices.

Kharis kidnaps Amina and drags her back to the deserted mining shack he shares with Yousef, their little love nest in Mapleton's gay ghetto, way outside the high-rent district, where they enjoy steeping their tana tea together. Once Yousef gets a load of Amina with her increasingly large white streaks, he decides to switch teams and steal his somewhat-dead roommate's girlfriend. Yousef thinks that sharing a tana cocktail with Amina would mean an eternal lifetime of hot necrophile nookie for himself. Kharis believes that, after waiting 3000 years, he has a prior claim on Ananka/Amina. (Amina/Ananka's opinions on the matter are not consulted.) Kharis carries Amina into one of the many quicksand-bestrewn swamps that Massachusetts would have if it were Louisiana. On the way, Amina turns into a withered ancient hag. Once at the bog, they sink together into the quicksand to die happily ever after, before the horrified eyes of Tom and a howling mob of villagers opposed to May-December romances between older men and women 3000 years their junior.

The next installment, *The Mummy's Curse*, was released a mere five months after *The Mummy's Ghost*. It turns out that Massachusetts *is* in Louisiana, because the movie begins with the draining of the Mapleton swamps and the uncovering of Kharis and Ananka's mummies, *in Louisiana!*

Either the screenwriters forgot that the two previous movies were set in Massachusetts, difficult to believe given that *Curse* was shooting while *Ghost* was in theaters, or they thought quicksand *flowed* about 2000 miles from Massachusetts to Louisiana's bayous (despite stagnant water being the essential ingredient in quicksand), or Kharis carried Ananka in his arms, pursued by Tom and the mob of villagers, for 2000 miles, all of them *on foot*, before sinking into the marsh, or no one connected with *The Mummy's Curse* gave a rat's ass about what they were doing. Which could it be? I'm stumped.

They establish that the mummy and his princess sank into the swamp twenty-five years before. That sets this movie fifty-five years after *The Mummy's Hand*, set back in 1940, yet the world, the clothes, the technology, the hairstyles, and the social attitudes in this picture in no way resemble 1995. No one even has a TV. No one ever says: "They can put a man on the moon but they can't kill one lousy mummy." No one's obsessing about the OJ Simpson trial. Some 1995 this is. In fact, the movie looks suspiciously like 1944.

A Professor Halsey from the "Scripps Museum" and his Egyptian "sidekick" Dr. Ilzor Zandaab, played by the always-lovely Peter Coe, arrive to reclaim the mummies from the swamp. Ilzor Zandaab, along with having an extremely peculiar name, even in a movie where the heroine is named "Amina Mansouri," wears a fez. We know what this means. Either he's a Shriner, a Son of the Desert, a Time Lord, or an Evil High Priest of Arkham. Well, he's not a Shriner nor a Son of the Desert, and with this movie's peculiar version of 1995, he's certainly no time traveler.

Sure enough, Ilzor has a sinister "sidekick" of his own, Ragheb, played by the always slimy and weasly Martin Kosleck. Ragheb has already retrieved Kharis and spirited him away to a handy, nearby ancient hilltop temple, one of the many ruins from ancient African civilizations that lie scattered across Louisiana.

Ilzor is also here to play matchmaker and reunite Kharis with Ananka, although, come to think of it, they were united when last we saw them and required no reuniting.

In an accidentally effective and creepy scene, Princess Ananka/Amina, played this time by wonderful Virginia Christine, a vastly more interesting actress than Ramsey Ames, wakes up and rises out of the dried dirt of the swamp, covered in filth, as the sun revives her, in a shot that makes your skin crawl as much for Virginia as it does for Amina.

Kharis carries Ananka off to the nearby temple. Virginia Christine told me, during a conversation we had in the late 1970s, the same thing most folks who worked with Chaney in the 1940s tell: that Lon was pretty much useless after he'd drunk his lunch each day. She told me about shooting the scene where Chaney had to carry her up the worn and uneven steps of the ancient Louisiana temple. She was actually strapped to Chaney by a canvas binding to aid him in holding her up.

Unfortunately, they were shooting this scene after lunch, and predictably, he slipped and fell on her. As if it was not bad enough having an enormous drunken man, fall on top of her, her being strapped to him at a right angle to him meant she could not crawl out from under him, nor could he be rolled off of her until the crew managed to cut her loose. The shots in the finished movie are of Eddie Parker carrying her up the steps while Chaney slept off his lunch in his dressing room.

While Kharis is crushing Ananka/Amina on the steps, Ragheb lures pretty young Betty Walsh (what—they didn't want to call her Zenobia Xylophone?) to the temple for a little eternal slap-and-tickle of his own. Betty is played by Kay Harding, an actress whose career was not as extensive as Peggy Moran's or Ramsey Ames', lasting barely a year and a half. After *The Mummy's Curse*, she went on to play the memorable role of "4th Victim" in *Sherlock Holmes and the Scarlet Claw*.

When her character was killed in that film, she took it seriously, and never acted in a movie again.

But Ilzor catches Ragheb sneaking Betty into the dorm, I mean temple, and is enraged to find his "sidekick" cheating on him with an actress playing almost her only role ever to have a proper name. (Among Kay's tiny handful of roles are such classic beloved characters as "Woman in Montage," "Information Girl," "Minor Role," "Student," and of course her signature character, "4th Victim.") "The curse of Amon-Ra upon you, Ragheb!" Ilzor snippily hisses, adding, "Your tongue shall be torn from your mouth for the vows you have sworn to falsely!" Well, he was very upset, so maybe we can forgive his scrambled syntax.

Ilzor has a solution to the embarrassing domestic squabble Betty is witnessing; Betty must die. Sounds reasonable, and it would be good research for her upcoming role as "4th Victim." Ragheb registers his objections to this plan by sinking a dagger into Ilzor's back. Ragheb's anger can shatter your spine.

Once Kharis, Ragheb, and Ilzor are all dead, Professor Halsey, the alleged hero of this movie on the rare occasions when he's on camera, finds Amina/Ananka now reverted to a withered ancient mummy. Rather than call a doctor, Halsey just states he will put her and Kharis into his museum, without so much as an autopsy for the poor, doomed girl. Given how temporary their deaths have proved in the past, I wouldn't want them in my museum. At best, I could wake up and find the state I live in, California, has suddenly become Louisiana. No thank you.

So one might reasonably expect that Kharis would rise again, as he had proved excessively resilient in the past, but Kharis did not return to movie screens for fifteen years, when Sir Christopher Lee played the titular role in Hammer's 1959 *The Mummy*, a better movie than any of the Universal Kharis movies. With his name (probably intentionally) misspelled as *Klaris*, and played full-time by Eddie Parker, the mummy would encounter Abbott & Costello in one of their lamest efforts, 1955's *Abbott & Costello Meet the Mummy*. (Even with Marie Windsor and Richard Deacon enlivening the cast, *A&C Meet the Mummy* is almost unwatchable, and I'm a lifelong A&C fan.) This miserable series of movies was mercifully over, and no one was happier about that than Lon Chaney Jr. Sometimes dead is better.

MUMMY'S BOYS

Turhan Bey was a tireless ladies man, and reputed to be one of the very best lays in 1940s Hollywood. No woman ever complained of bad sex with Turhan. I found him charming, suave, and intelligent when I talked with him via phone (I was in Los Angeles; he was in Paris) in 1974.

Forty years after leaving Hollywood and returning home to Vienna, where he worked as a photographer, Turhan came back to Hollywood, now bald as an egg and no longer the dark-eyed dreamboat he was in the decade before my birth, and acted for a few more years on TV, including appearances on *Murder, She Wrote*, *SeaQuest DSV*, and *Babylon 5*. He died in 2012 at the age of 90.

Robert Lowry, who played Tom Hervey, the hero of *The Mummy's Ghost*, achieved a small dose of superhero immortality in 1949, when he became the second Bruce Wayne / Batman, in the horrible theatrical serial *Batman and Robin*, opposite *House of Dracula*'s Jane Addams as Vicki Vale.

Lowry also appeared in an episode of the TV series *The Adventures of Superman* with George Reeves, titled "The Deadly Rock," resulting in the first meeting of a Superman and a Batman, although Lowry wasn't playing Bruce Wayne.

9

TWO ZOMBIES, STRAIGHT UP
White Zombie (1932)
I Walked with a Zombie (1943)

> *There's no beauty here, only death and decay.*
> — Paul Holland (Tom Conway), losing his job on the West Indies tourism board in *I Walked with a Zombie.*

"What about zombies?" you ask. Although a movie and TV staple today, more common than cockroaches, with their own TV series as well as invading the works of Jane Austin, there were only two important zombie movies in the 1930s and 1940s, though zombies did show up in comedies like *The Ghost Breakers* and *Zombies on Broadway*.

White Zombie, despite the classy-sounding racist title, is a dreadful, turgid piece of claptrap. It looks great, like the first three reels of *Dracula* drawn out to feature length. Bela Lugosi at his hammiest (and no one, not even Curly Howard of the Three Stooges, was hammier than Lugosi at his hammiest) stars as a wizard in the West Indies who employs zombies as a cheap labor force (thus making its metaphor slavery) and as a Cosby-ish means of seduction. The rest of the cast appears to have been chosen so as to make Lugosi come across like Laurence Olivier. Bela actually gives the best performance in the film, and he's embarrassing. By all means watch it, but leave the sound off and invent your own plot and dialogue. You'll be improving it no matter what you come up with.

At the opposite end of the quality spectrum, RKO's *I Walked with a Zombie* is, in spite of the hilariously lurid title, a *great* movie, possibly the best movie discussed in this book, except for *Bride of Frankenstein*. Produced by the brilliant Val Lewton, directed by Jacques Touneur, and written by Ardel Wray and Curt Siodmak (who resisted his usual penchant for putting brain transplants into everything he wrote), it's really a very loose adaptation of *Jane Eyre* set in the West Indies. It features a literate screenplay, black-and-white photography so gorgeous it can make Technicolor look drab, and a fine cast, including Tom Conway, Francis Dee, and Edith Barrett, who, at the time, was Mrs. Vincent Price. It is classic gothic cinema at its best.

THE LIVING DEAD QUIZ

(33% of your grade. Answers at the back of the book.)

1. Bram Stoker, author of the novel *Dracula*, had a very prominent day job for a very famous boss. What was that job and who was his boss?

2. Before marrying Bram Stoker, iron-willed Florence Stoker was proposed to by one of the most important figures of 19th century English literature. Who was her unsuccessful suitor and did she make the right choice?

3. Mrs. Stoker extended her iron will into trying to have a great movie based, without credit, on her husband's work destroyed. Fortunately, she failed. What is this great film?

4. In addition to Lon Chaney and Conrad Veidt, another actor, fairly forgotten today, was almost cast as Dracula, instead of Lugosi. This actor went on to another role (that would eventually be taken by the best Dracula of all, Sir Christopher Lee), playing the henchman for a great horror icon. Who was the actor, what was the other role, and who was the horror icon he henched for?

5. *The Mummy* has been officially remade thrice so far. Who played the title role and the hero in each of these two films?

PART TWO
It's a Mad, Mad, Mad, Mad Science!

> *He meddled in things man should leave alone.*
> — Dr. Arthur Kemp (William Harrigan), spouting a beloved cliché in *The Invisible Man*.

Back in the 20th century, when dinosaurs still roamed the earth, they had a thing called "science." This odd, intellectual misstep was practiced by "scientists," a strange cult of evil high priests who believed in the false god of "reason," and who felt we needed television, cell phones, medicine, and moon rocks.

In our far more enlightened 21st century, various forces of ignorance attempt to completely discredit "science," and it's evil false beliefs like "history," "physics," and "common sense." This has made many scientists mad. Therefore, our nation is plagued by an enormous cabal of grudge-bearing mad scientists, trying to make us believe in nonsense like climate change and natural selection.

Fortunately cinema, the great educator, has furnished us with cautionary movies about mad scientists, all with the same essential message: "Knowledge is bad." In fact, even the act of reading, or at least reading something other than the Bible, is suspect. Everything humanity really needed to know was already known back in the Bronze Age. You should stop reading this book right now and throw it away, just to be safe.

10

IN THE BEGINNING, HENRY CREATED MAN
Frankenstein (1931)

Oh, in the name of God, now I know what it feels like to be God!
— Henry Frankenstein (Colin Clive), being modest

The Story

Brilliant but high-strung medical student Henry Frankenstein and his posture-challenged "sidekick" Fritz are experimentinf in the artificial creation of human life. They rob graves, raid unattended gallows, and steal an unused criminal's brain from the local university, stitching together a patchwork corpse which they imbue with life. The innocent creature, mistreated by the sadistic Fritz and abandoned by its creator, escapes from the lab,and goes on a killing spree. When it accidentally drowns a little girl, Henry postpones his wedding to lead a torch-bearing mob in pursuit of the monster. They confront one another in an old mill where the monster tosses Henry off a balcony and then is burned to death in the mill by a mob. Henry survives his fall and marries his neglected fiancée.

The Production

Dracula had been a huge hit for Universal, so in the broiling summer of 1931, *Frankenstein* was rushed into production. The direction was assigned to and then yanked from the over-praised Robert Florey, who had recently done a lousy job of co-directing the Marx Brothers' first sound film, *The Cocoanuts*.

The silent role of the monster was haughtily refused by Bela Lugosi, thus paving the way not only for Karloff, but assuring

Jane Wyman that she wouldn't have to compete with Lugosi for her Oscar-winning mute role in *Johnny Belinda*. Author Gregory William Mank quotes Lugosi as saying, "I will not be a grunting, babbling idiot for anybody! ... I need a part where I can *act*!"

The direction was handed to the openly gay English genius James Whale. Whale immediately proved his genius by almost literally plucking Boris Karloff from the crowd to replace Lugosi in the role of the monster, and, as it turned out to Lugosi's everlasting ire, also as Universal's number-one bogeyman. Karloff instantly saw that the monster *was* a part where he could *act*, and act it he did, right into the hearts and the dark bedroom corners of America, while the resulting movie set the Frankenstein myth in concrete for all time to come.

Dwight Frye and Edward Van Sloan were drafted from the *Dracula* cast for similar roles, while David Manners was replaced in the romantic support role by the even duller, if somewhat more masculine, John Boles. Bette Davis was briefly considered for Elizabeth, but Carl Laemmle thought she was ugly (well, he was getting along in years; perhaps his eyes were going), so the part went to Mae Clark, who was pretty and talented, but no Bette Davis. Clark's greatest claim to fame would come that same year when James Cagney used her face for a fruit juicer in *The Public Enemy*.

What's Good About It

Almost everything. Shot only ten months after *Dracula*, *Frankenstein* is a vastly better movie. Brilliantly directed by Whale, gorgeously designed by Whale, Jack Pierce, Charles D. Hall, and Herman Rosse, magnificently photographed by Arthur Edeson, who would go on to shoot *The Maltese Falcon* and *Casablanca*, well-acted by all, except arguably Edward Van Sloan, John Boles, and Mae Clark, and featuring Boris Karloff giving one of the greatest acting performances in the history of American cinema, *Frankenstein* holds up as a still-great movie.

Karloff's monster is a pathetic innocent with a nasty temper. Nightmarishly scary-looking? You bet. But also loveable from his first entrance, almost halfway through the film. And damn if he isn't even kind of sexy in a primitive brute sort of way.

THE LAST MAN

Frankenstein, or the Modern Prometheus was not Mary Shelley's only science-fiction novel. There is also *The Last Man*, Mary's 1826 novel relating the end of mankind, wiped off the earth by a plague in the 21st century. Try not to panic. Mary was very depressed when she wrote it. This is a woman who literally kept her late husband's heart around the house in a jar as a gruesomely sentimental souvenir.

Jules Verne and H.G. Wells were both serious science enthusiasts. Science itself did not interest Mary much. She was far from a futurist. Her 21st century in *The Last Man* is advanced technologically beyond 1826 by about ten minutes. Apparently, it did not occur to her that stuff would get invented. According to Mary, we in the 21st century still get about on horses. She does see the American Civil war coming, but gets the outcome wrong when she introduces the ambassador from the "Northern States of America." *Frankenstein, or the Modern Prometheus* is also science-light and depression-heavy. Mary had a rather unhappy life, and it shows in her work.

What's Bad About It
In the few scenes of Henry's fiancée Elizabeth fretting with her back-up boyfriend, Victor Moritz (John Boles), and fending off the grumblings of Henry's tiresome old fool of a father, Baron Frankenstein (Frederick Kerr), one can feel James Whale's interest plummet, and the movie becomes dull for a very few minutes, but once it's gone back to its grotesques, the picture resurrects like the monster in a thunderstorm.

Edward Van Sloan is as pompous and smug as always, but his role here, as the university professor for whom Henry's experiment represents the best science fair project of all time, is considerably reduced, and the monster wins our hearts by strangling him.

What's Gay About It
Everything! To me, *Frankenstein* is the gayest horror story of all, a tale of a man who ignores his fiancée and eschews heterosexual reproduction in order to make life with another man in a hideaway far from prying eyes, building himself a superhunk who almost kills his girlfriend for him. (He *does* kill her in Mary Shelley's great novel.)

Frankenstein lends itself to many interpretations. Breeders may find themselves properly horrified by the hideous spectacle of a man defying God, perverting the natural order, and suffering the deserved fate that all must suffer who *turn their back*, so to speak, on "normal" sex. Feminists like Mary Shelley's mother may see it as a story of what happens when men try to cut women out of the reproductive loop. I, however, prefer to view the Frankenstein Follies as a gay parable, whether one identifies with the monster, a misunderstood societal outcast who just wants to be loved; the hunchbacked assistant, an unattractive troll and bungler basking in the protection of the handsome older man who spends far more time with him than with his girlfriend; or the mad scientist himself, who'd rather make boys with other boys, and who only wants to eradicate death. Is that so wrong?

The biological purpose of sex, as the religious right will tell you before clubbing you to death in God's name, is reproduction. Well, Hank and Fritz, in their love nest/lab in a ruined old phallic watchtower, merge their organs, turn on their equipment, generate wild electricity, and create life together, bringing into existence Hank's monstrous son, while Hank's girlfriend, her alternate boyfriend, and his skeptical old professor, are forced to just sit and *watch*! In orgasmic ecstasy, Henry shrieks, "It's alive! It's alive! Oh, in the name of God, now I know what it's like to be God!"

Was James Whale aware of the gay overtones in the movie he was making? Of course he was. Tod Browning may have missed the homosexual implications of *Dracula*, but Whale was completely aware of what he was doing, and amusing himself greatly in the process. Who did he cast as his hero? A man he'd directed before, both onscreen and on stage, Colin Clive, a tormented, alcoholic gay man married to a lesbian.

Henry and Fritz go out together evenings to dig up men, albeit dead ones, and finding cold swingers at the hot local gallows, always seeking out guys with the freshest and largest organs. As usual, there's more than a mild whiff of necrophilia.

Fritz's idea of fun turns out to be tormenting the monster with vicious S&M bondage games involving chains and burning faggots, down in his dungeon-playroom, but the monster plays too rough and kills Fritz, not realizing that "aaaaaah!" was Fritz's safe word.

Henry's father disapproves of his son having an occupation. "Humph! Pretty sorts of experiments these must be!" Dad snorts with withering sarcasm at the mention of his son's work. That sounds familiar. While Henry is delirious, Poppa throws a giant wedding together in record time, wrongly concluding that some marital bliss is just what the doctor would order if he weren't out of his mind.

Once loose, the monster kills the very first female he ever meets. He's less than a week old and he's already killed three people. I think someone needs a nap.

A howling mob of outraged villagers, recognizing the basic unnatural monstrousness of the living product of homosexual union, his murder of a child proving him a threat to *the family*, pursues the monster, probably chanting "save the children" as they do. Henry uses the hunt for his wayward boy as an excuse to ditch his wedding. Victor pretends to want to go along on the hunt, but is easily dissuaded when Henry basically hands Elizabeth over to Victor, who has been hanging around through the whole movie for just that purpose. Victor bravely makes no further attempt to join the hunt.

Aftermath

Frankenstein was an even bigger hit than *Dracula*, which makes sense, as it is so very much better. It may not frighten anyone any more, but I suspect that today's ten year olds may still find themselves haunted by it as strongly as I was. *Frankenstein* is so great, it's almost impossible to believe that its sequel is a whole lot better, but it is.

WHO'S YOUR DADDY?

Frederick Kerr, who played the crotchety old Baron Frankenstein, was the grandfather of actor John Kerr of *South Pacific*. John was born the very month *Frankenstein* was released. In the 1956 homosexual problem drama *Tea & Sympathy*, he was tormented at college for seeming gay, which the movie *clearly* states, even though he was really straight. This, of course, implies that if he were gay, making his life a living hell would be perfectly fine, just what he deserves. The movie and the play it is based on are passionate pleas for tolerance for not-very-masculine heterosexuals.

John Kerr was also the victim of Vincent Price's swishing pendulum in *The Pit and the Pendulum*. A highly intelligent man, Kerr eventually left acting and became a lawyer. He died in 2013, and none of his obituaries called him the "Grandson of Frankenstein." So, was the monster his cousin?

11

THE MATING GAME
Bride of Frankenstein (1935)

I love dead; hate living.
— Frankenstein's monster (Boris Karloff),
being an out-and-proud necrophiliac

You're wise in your generation.
— Dr. Pretorius (Ernest Thesiger),
being supportive and accepting

It's no exaggeration to say that I'm writing this whole book just to write this chapter. In my book, *Bride of Frankenstein* is the greatest movie ever made, and as this *is* my book, the prosecution rests.

And if you don't accept that it is the greatest movie ever made, since "pistols at dawn" is not a viable response, perhaps you can at least admit it's one of the *gayest* movies ever made. Next to *Bride of Frankenstein*, *Brokeback Mountain* is a Russ Meyer movie. ("Brokeback Vixens"?)

The Story

On a dark and stormy night, Lord Byron asks Mary Shelley to entertain Percy Shelley and himself by relating what happened after *Frankenstein* ended. Fortunately for them, she has a sequel all plotted out and ready to tell. "That wasn't the end at all," she says.

The monster survives the burning mill when he falls through the floor into a subterranean pond. Henry Frankenstein, now Baron Frankenstein, marries Elizabeth, but on their wedding night Henry's old gay professor, Septimus Pretorius, drops by and proposes jointly building a mate for the monster, since the first experiment turned out so well.

The monster is captured by a mob, escapes, and hides out in a blind man's cabin in the woods, where he learns to speak, until passing hunters flush him out. Taking refuge in a tomb, the monster meets Dr. Pretorius, who seduces him. When Henry gets cold feet, Septimus has the monster kidnap Elizabeth, forcing Henry to participate in the unholy project. The female creature is brought to life, but when she sees the monster, she is repulsed. The monster blows up the lab, killing all except Henry and Elizabeth, who escape to breed sequels. We don't return to Mary Shelley, but I imagine Lord Byron enjoyed it.

The Production

Frankenstein had made tons of money, but it still took Universal four years to get James Whale to commit to shooting what was first called *The Return of Frankenstein*. Whale felt he'd wrung the story dry in his 71-minute movie. Eventually, Whale noticed that by taking almost nothing from the book beyond the premise, along with the name of the hero, Victor, for the hero's best friend, and the name of the best friend, Henry, for the name of the hero, he still had a whole lot of story left over, just lying around fallow in the great novel.

Whale, John Balderston, and William Hurlbut went skimming through Mary Shelley's novel and selected a few prime plot tidbits to build their story around. Whale kept boredom at bay by turning his horror extravaganza into a spectacular gay black comedy, the story of a blind date between two reanimated cadavers, the biggest necrophile romance until *Laura*.

Karloff, Colin Clive, and Dwight Frye returned, Frye as a new twisted assistant named Karl, since Fritz had died halfway through *Frankenstein*. Elizabeth is now played by beautiful, 17-year-old Valerie Hobson.

There is a new burgomaster played by delightfully pompous E.E. Clive, who had just played a similar role in Whale's *The Invisible Man*. He has a mustache so large it looks to be half of his body weight. Also imported from the *Invisible Man* cast is the shrill, hilarious Una O'Conner as Minnie, the maid whom the burgomaster warns not to riot. "We want no rioting. No riots." Mind you, he has just officiated over an ugly lynch mob burning a man alive, but that still doesn't mean he wants Minnie screeching in his ear.

The *fabulous* Ernst Thesiger steals the whole movie as Dr. Septimus Pretorius, a waspy, effeminate pouf of a mad scientist. Ernest was as big an old queen as ever entered a sound stage. He was a close friend of Whale's, and had already displayed his acidly camp comic persona in Whale's *The Old Dark House*. Whale wanted Thesiger for Pretorius—the role is clearly written for him—precisely to make Pretorius as overtly homosexual as he could get away with in 1935.

Thesiger, who was married, but not seriously, had once authored a book entitled *Adventures in Embroidery*, and actually used to refer to himself as the "Stitchin' Bitch." He was the companion of queens and Queens, as he was a crony of England's Queen Mother, with whom he would sit, both doing needlepoint, as he amused her with his wicked gossip.

I think it's a measure of Whale's sly wit that he casts real life gay men as the normal humans, and confirmed breeders Karloff and Dwight Frye as the monster and hunchback.

At the top of the camp casting heap stands supreme Elsa Lanchester, Charles Laughton's beard, hired to play the monster's beard and to double as Mary Shelley.

Franz Waxman contributed a great musical score as well, much of which got recycled in the *Flash Gordon* movie serials.

What's Good About It

Everything! Scripts, sets, costumes, make-up, acting, photography, and best of all, directing.

Whale emphasized the story's literary roots with a gorgeous gothic prologue in which Mary Shelley, played by Elsa in a fantastically expensive gown that the real Mary could never have afforded, is persuaded to improvise *Frankenstein*'s sequel. She impressively ad-libs a story that took a top director and two fine writers months to craft.

Of course, the real Byron and Shelley, bisexual advocates of free love, with Percy Shelley being also a prominent atheist, were simply too free-thinking for the thought police at the Breen Office ever to allow to be portrayed accurately, or to express the ideas they really had, ideas the Breen Office was deeply invested in ruthlessly suppressing, so they are instead depicted as effete, effeminate ponces, who prattle bellicose poppycock as they blow smoke up each other's asses. Byron labels himself as "England's Greatest Sinner," though no hint of what his sins may be are given. "But I can not flatter myself to that extent," he says, after flattering himself to that extent. Byron describes the monster as "so fearful, so horrible, that only a half-crazed brain could have devised," which seems a rather rude thing to say to Mary's face.

When the bride is finally unwrapped, Septimus announces her as "the bride of Frankenstein." Wedding bells ring. The orchestra plays the melody of Rogers & Hammerstein's *Bali Hai* a decade before Rogers wrote it, and it is all a grand, serio-comic vision of insane magnificence, the apotheosis of the Laemmles' horror visions, the summit of Whale's gothic Everest. The most disturbing aspect of it all is that, with all her scars and weirdness, Elsa's bride is beautiful. As Emory says in *The Boys in the Band*, "Oh, Mary, it takes a fairy to make something pretty." Pauline Kael wrote of Elsa's monster bride, "She won our hearts forever, as Margaret Hamilton did as the wicked witch."

What's Bad About It
Nothing!

What's Gay About It
What isn't? Let's start with Dr. Pretorius, as overtly a gay character as you'll find in a 1930s movie not played by Franklin Pangborn. Elizabeth has spoken the magic words: "We are not meant to know those things." (Says who, Liz?) We have hit the defining phrase of mad science: things man was not meant to know. Bad knowledge, *bad*! Elizabeth clearly fails to see why, if Henry wants to create life so badly, he doesn't just give her one, and let her pop out a Frankenstein Jr the old-fashioned way. Cue Pretorius.

Minnie describes Pretorius as "a very queer-looking old gentleman" when he arrives to lure Henry Frankenstein out of his marital bed, literally, and away from his fiancée, to make babies the unnatural way with him. Not much ambiguity there.

Hank puts up some token resistance. "*Never!* This is outrageous! I'm through with it! I'll have no more of this hellspawn! As soon as I'm well I'm to be married and I'm going away." How often have I heard *that* speech? All he leaves out is, "Besides, I was so drunk I can't remember a thing."

"Don't put it so crudely," Septimus says, rightly ignoring Hank's nonsensical protestations. "I have ventured to hope that you and I together...might *probe* the mysteries of Life and Death, and reach a goal undreamed of by science."

Thesiger's Pretorius could make Grady Sutton look butch. "Do have a little gin. It is my *only* weakness," Pretorius lies, and then he proposes the famous toast, "To a new world of gods and monsters."

(Thesiger had already established "It is my only weakness" as his catchphrase back in *The Old Dark House*. It's reappearance here constitutes an in-joke reference to the earlier movie.)

Then Septimus displays the *fruits* of his own non-heterosexual life-making. "My experiments did not turn out quite like yours, Henry, but science, like love, has her little surprises," says Septimus, making the perverted-sex/perverted-science connection as explicit as possible in a 1935 movie.

Septimus propositions Henry. "Leave the charnel house and follow the lead of nature, or God if you like your Bible stories," he says, sounding almost like a Christian fundamentalist preacher until you notice the contempt in his voice at the mention of "your Bible stories." (Septimus can get away with being an atheist in the movie because he's considered the villain, despite being the most loveable character in the picture.) "Be fruitful and multiply. Create a race, a man-made race, upon the face of the earth. Why not?" Septimus is a Mad Big Thinker. He's gone far beyond merely wanting to cure death. He wants to mate cadavers to make baby cadavers in a mad orgy of fecund heterosexual necrophilia. He truly wants to play God. "Alone, you have a created a man," says Septimus. "Now, *together*, we shall create his mate!"

"You mean..." trails off Henry, unable to bring himself to finish the distasteful thought.

"Yes, a woman. That should be really interesting," Pretorious replies. The scene fades out at this point, so we can only imagine how they begin their partnership.

The mob captures the monster and crucifies him on a pole. As the monster hangs there, suffering, pelted with rocks by the jeering mob, looking like a still from *The Passion of the Monster*, there's no doubt whatever where Whale places the audience's sympathy. The defenders of the normal are seen as the truly vicious monsters while the poor miserable deviant is barbarously gay bashed. (Yes, there's also abundant Christ imagery linked to the resurrected monster throughout the movie, but that's a whole other Golgotha of beans.)

When the monster escapes again into the woods, he finally finds the acceptance and love he seeks in a homo-romantic tryst with a blind man who, not being a looksist, instantly falls for the big hunk of inarticulate muscle.

Blind Man, played by O.P. Higgie, who played Nayland Smith in the Warner Oland Fu Manchu movies, babbles on about the life they're going to have together, "I will look after you, and you will *comfort* me." They've known each other precisely two and a half minutes—I timed it—and Blind Man is already picking out china patterns. At *exactly* two minutes and forty-two seconds into their relationship, in an unbroken scene, Blind Man is tucking Monster into his bed! And I thought *I* was a slut.

Then comes the most salacious shot in the whole movie. Blind Man prays tearfully, thanking God for finally sending him a "companion," which he's wanted for a *long time*. You get me? Blind Man then breaks down in tears of joy, bending over the bed to cry, his face zeroing right in on the monster's monstrous crotch! This didn't happen by accident. James Whale set this shot up, and he did it deliberately.

The camera then cuts to a reverse angle from behind Blind Man, so it is no longer possible to see that he isn't going down on the monster, and Blind Man sobs, causing his head and shoulders to bob up and down rhythmically. Completing the illusory image, Monster moans, convulsively grips Blind Man's shoulder, rolls his head back and whimpers. And from a small crucifix on the wall above the bed, tiny Jesus watches all of this. Apparently deciding he wants out of this shot, Jesus vanishes off the cross (I'm not joking; look at the shot) as the shot fades, with Whale emphasizing this as he leaves the cross itself glowing in the shot after all else, including tiny Jesus, has faded away.

This is what happens when you watch these movie with a really dirty mind like mine.

When we rejoin the blissful boys it is several days, perhaps even weeks, later. Blind Man has been teaching Monster to speak and to appreciate plain food, cheap wine, a cancerous smoke, and the pleasure of amiable companionship. Blind Man has Monster feel his log and tells him, "This is wood." Monster enjoys feeling Blind Man's wood. Wood good. Fire no good.

Monster has developed a love of music and the two are on the verge of getting season tickets to the opera together when their ecstatic idyll comes to a crashing end, predictably by their being discovered together by representatives of the "normal" world, in this case two hunters, one of them John Carradine. The hunters get a gander at these two men, one blind, the other a walking corpse, and recognize a threat to straight marriage when they see one. They have a shrieking attack of homosexual panic and quickly reduce the cottage to a flaming hell. The boys were happy. Who were they hurting?

Back at the tower lab, Septimus muses, "It is interesting to think, Henry, that once upon a time we should have been burnt at the stake as wizards for this experiment," as though the authorities would smile at it now. Septimus also says, "The human heart is more complex than any other part of the body." Apparently he's never heard of the brain.

You want sex? Wait till you see them "lower the Cosmic Diffuser," a large, unmistakably phallic construct that goes up and down in the vaginal lab, shooting at the female fetus balls of sparkly electrical sperm, gathered from the lightning via the two testicular kites. This creation scene, which far outdoes the one in *Frankenstein*, is fantasy sex on a spectacular scale, and the only woman present is dead—at first.

And so life comes to Elsa Lanchester's monster bride, a fruit fly for a gay monster, memorably coiffured, undoubtedly by Pretorius. It's always looked to me like Elsa gets immediate hots for Henry. Elsa's marital history does suggest that she'd home in on the nearest gay man, anyway. What is not in doubt is that she's utterly repulsed by Monster. (This sometimes happens with arranged marriages.) Monster wants her, she wants Henry, and Septimus wants to watch.

When I met Elsa Lanchester in 1968, I told her the scene looked like a deranged episode of *The Dating Game* in which the contestant picked Bachelor #1 only to find once she saw them that she vastly preferred Bachelor #3. Miss Lanchester laughed merrily and said, "I think we made a real minor classic there." I told her I'd remove the word "minor" from that evaluation. I may have babbled a bit, as I was delirious and a bit giddy to find myself, at age 18, standing in a buffet line at a party, chatting with the star of my favorite movie.

Anyway, as often happens when gay people try to repress their true nature and live straight, the match-making is a catastrophe. And really, Pretorius, Elizabeth, and the bride are all lusting for Henry. He is nice looking I suppose, but he's hardly hot enough for all this attention. Frankly, Monster is still the man in the room with the most sexual heat going on, Dwight Frye's Karl being dead by this point, but Monster's advances are again met with screams.

Rejected once too often, Monster reaches for the lever that will blow up the joint. (Why do they have such a lever? Does that seem like a good idea to you? What if the cat jumped on it?) Monster, Bride, and Septimus have a date, a four-way with Death. Monster then takes after his dad a bit and plays a little God himself. (Why not? Whale's been putting him in shots with crucifixes and other Christ iconography throughout the movie.) "Yes! Go! You live! Go!" he shouts to Henry and Elizabeth, who has just arrived to pay a surprise visit to her husband's love nest. "You stay," Monster snarls at Septimus, who led him on. "We belong dead." Before he pulls the lever, Bride hisses at Monster one last time, and he looks at her with tears in his eyes. She's broken his oversized heart, and Karl is too dead to go fetch him a fresh one.

Aftermath

The last shots of *Bride of Frankenstein* are of Henry and Elizabeth watching the phallic tower explode orgasmically and then collapse into a flaccid pile of rubble. (The buffet dinner where I had my chat with Elsa Lanchester actually took place on Stage 28, the very Universal soundstage where that final model shot of the tower collapsing, and the opening shot of Lord Byron's chateau in a thunderstorm, were shot.) It would be four years before a new studio regime would pump cinematic Viagra back into that tower. The next film in the series, *Son of Frankenstein*, is pretty damn good, but nothing could truly top Carl Laemmle Jr. And James Whale's masterpiece. Whale didn't even try. He never made another fantasy movie.

VALERIE HOBSON'S CHOICE

Follow this game of Six Degrees of Frankenstein closely. Later on, after a film career that saw her play Estella in David Lean's great film of Dickens' *Great Expectations*, and Joan Greenwood's romantic rival in the brilliant black comedy *Kind Hearts and Coronets*, Valerie Hobson married British politician John Profumo, who became prime minister of England. Then in the 1960s, Profumo was caught up in a huge sex scandal involving his cheating on Valerie with a "party girl" (a lovely euphemism for whore) named Christine Keeler. The scandal toppled the Profumo government. (This is what comes of letting straight people run the government.) Hobson, despite the deep, almost unfathomable public humiliation, chose to stay loyal to her husband, and never divorced him.

In the 1980s, a movie about the Profumo scandal, imaginatively titled *Scandal*, was made, in which John Profumo was played by the great gay actor Sir Ian McKellan. A decade later, Sir Ian was nominated for an Oscar he should have won for playing James Whale in the great movie *Gods and Monsters*, which contained flashback re-creations of Whale directing *Bride of Frankenstein*, which, to return to the start of this circle, starred Valerie Hobson in technically the title role, since it is she who married Henry Frankenstein. The movie is *not* titled *Bride of the Monster*. That turkey starred Bela Lugosi.

12

THE KING OF BLOOD
Boris Karloff (1887–1969)

> *He nothing common did, or mean,*
> *Upon that memorable scene.*
> — Inscription on a memorial plaque
> for Boris Karloff in London

The words of the above quote are inscribed on a plaque in St. Paul's Church, Covent Garden, London, in memory of a British actor who was both a gentleman and a gentle man, and who achieved undying worldwide fame and affection under the self-created stage name Boris Karloff.

Of the seven supreme iconic horror stars, the Chaneys, Karloff, Lugosi, Vincent Price, Peter Cushing, and Sir Christopher Lee, Karloff is unquestionably number one, the "King of Blood," as he refers to himself in the movie *Targets*.

In the amazingly ongoing Karloff vs Lugosi acting debate, the attentive reader will have long since worked out that I fall squarely into the Karloff camp. I favor Karloff over Lugosi because, based on my own viewing of a large number of their respective movies, including all eight of their joint films, Karloff seems to me, by far, the better actor. I have never seen him run riotously over-the-top, out-of-control, on camera, as Lugosi so often did.

Not that Boris Karloff always gave a great performance. In 1958, Boris shot ten episodes of an anthology fantasy TV series for Hal Roach titled *The Veil*. Like his great later TV series, *Thriller*, Boris hosted all the episodes, and acted in some of them. The series was never sold, never broadcast, and Boris was never paid, a fact he never forgot. It has, however, come out on DVD. In one episode, "The Crystal Ball," Boris played

André Giraud, a charming French roué. Imagine Boris playing Maurice Chevalier's role in *Gigi* and you have his André Giraud. He's laughable in the role. It's an embarrassment. And he was also terrible in...ah...I'm sorry. I can't come up with a second example.

Boris was born William Henry Pratt, the youngest of nine siblings, on November 23, 1887, in Camberwell, a suburb of London. Boris's great-aunt, the sister of his mother's mother, was Anna Leonowens, the "Anna" in the novel *Anna and the King of Siam* and in Rogers & Hammerstein's *The King and I*.

Boris' mother was half-Indian, and his Asian heritage showed in his perpetual tan. Out of make-up, Boris had a very dark skin, too dark for a pleasant boyhood in conservative 19th century England. His father deserting his family when Boris was five didn't help either. His mother's death two years later made matters still worse.

Billy Pratt, as he was known, was groomed for a diplomatic career, but he was infected with the acting bug at a young age, so at twenty-one he sailed off to Canada to seek a theatrical career far enough from England to avoid disgracing the family.

His earliest known film performance was in a 1919 Douglas Fairbanks film called *His Majesty, The American*. He worked on and off in films thereafter, his swarthy complexion often getting him cast as American Indians, Indian Indians, and Arabs. He was befriended by Lon Chaney, who told him, "The secret of success in Hollywood lies in being different from everyone else. Find something no one else can or will do, and they'll begin to take notice of you." Karloff certainly took this advice.

It was roles in two early classic crime melodramas, *Scarface* and *The Criminal Code*, that caught Whale's eye and led to Karloff being cast as the monster in *Frankenstein*, catapulting him to major stardom. Prior to November 1931, he was unknown. In 1932, he had his name above the title as he played the mute, brute butler in Whale's hilarious black comedy, *The Old Dark House*, Sax Rohmer's Chinese super-villain in the incredibly camp racist MGM thriller *The Mask of Fu Manchu*, and the austere, elderly Imhotep in *The Mummy*, an unprecedented display of versatility which cemented him as Hollywood's head bogeyman.

A classic Hollywood liberal, Boris was one of the original founders of the Screen Actors Guild, holding early planning meetings in intense secrecy in his own home at great personal and professional risk. His SAG membership card number had only a single digit.

Boris, like Bela Lugosi, was married five times. In a TV interview, his only child, the charming and intelligent Sarah Jane Karloff, said in reference to the end of her parents' marriage, "I don't have the faintest clue what went wrong. But at the same time, he married my stepmother the day after the divorce was final." Nope, there's nothing "faint" about that clue.

Boris was a homebody who loved doggies, gardening, and cricket. By all accounts, he was a kindly, gentle, generous man. No man who knew him ever had a bad word to say about him, except perhaps Bela Lugosi when he was in a foul mood, and Lugosi's son disputes even that. But does one show one's nastier side to one's own son? Many a Lugosi co-star testified to Bela's bitter assessment of Karloff.

Along with maintaining a career as a major movie star, he regularly returned to the Broadway stage, giving acclaimed performances in *Arsenic and Old Lace*, *The Lark*, *The Linden Tree*, *On Borrowed Time*, and as Captain Hook in *Peter Pan*.

Along with the aforementioned *The Veil*, some of his other 1950s TV work is available on DVD these days, including his playing Colonel Kurtz opposite Roddy McDowell in a bizarre live TV play adaptation of Conrad's *Heart of Darkness* (a role he plays entirely shirtless, despite being in his 70s), re-creating his Broadway performance in *Arsenic and Old Lace* opposite Tony Randall, and playing King Arthur in two different adaptations of Mark Twain's *A Connecticut Yankee in King Arthur's Court*, one of them being a cut-down version of the Broadway musical, in which Karloff sings a Rogers & Hart song. (Karloff sang on Broadway in *Peter Pan*. He's no Freddie Mercury, but he can carry a tune.)

Karloff's career resurgence in the 1960s resulted in fresh movies, the delightful comedies: *The Raven* and *The Comedy of Terrors*, both with Vincent Price and Peter Lorre;, the incoherent mess *The Terror*; the terrible H.P. Lovecraft adaptation *Die, Monster, Die!*; the idiotic beach movie *The Ghost in the Invisible*

Bikini; the Man from U.N.C.L.E. rip-off spy thriller *The Venetian Affair*; the quite interesting British thriller *The Sorcerers*; and a role co-starring with his London next-door neighbor and most-famous successor in the role of Frankenstein's monster, Sir Christopher Lee, in *The Curse of the Crimson Altar*.

In a wonderful irony, Karloff made four movies with the other great Hungarian bogeyman, the brilliant Peter Lorre, *You'll Find Out*, *The Bogeyman Will Get You*, *The Raven*, and *The Comedy of Terrors*, and each of those four movies is a comedy.

Two roles that stand out on the final page of his resumé are his narrating the animated TV version of Dr. Seuss's *How The Grinch Stole Christmas*, as well as supplying the voice of the Grinch (a vastly better treatment of the material than the wretched Jim Carrey vehicle), and as horror actor Byron Orlock in Peter Bogdanovich's directorial debut, the thoroughly excellent *Targets*.

In *Targets*, Boris essentially played himself, a horror star at the end of his career, who feels that the horrors of the day-to-day headlines now far eclipsed his elegant literary terrors, only to confront and disarm a psychotic sniper-killer at a drive-in theater playing his real-life lame movie *The Terror*. It's a well-written, first-rate thriller, a fine respectable coda for his career.

Only the body of Boris Karloff died on February 2, 1969. His work and his spirit will never die. In *Son of Frankenstein*, Lugosi's Ygor says to Basil Rathbone's Wolf von Frankenstein of Karloff's monster, "He can not be destroyed, can not die. Your father made him live for alvays." Bela never spoke truer words.

13

SIBLING RIVALRY
Son of Frankenstein (1939)

> He is my friend. He—he does things for me.
> — Ygor (Bela Lugosi),
> declaring his love for the monster

The Story

Many years after *Bride of Frankenstein*, Henry and Elizabeth von Frankenstein's (their name has acquired a "von" it didn't have before and won't have again) older son Wolf, his wife Elsa, and their excruciatingly annoying young son Peter, travel to their ancestral home in the village of Frankenstein (though they'd lived in Goldstadt, a corruption of "Ingolstadt," the Swiss city that is one of the primary settings of the novel, back in *Frankenstein*), to claim his baronial inheritance, only to be met with hostility by the bitter villagers, and to be offered protection by sinister Inspector Krogh, whose arm was torn off by the monster when Krogh was a boy.

Wolf also meets Ygor, a shepherd who was ineffectually hanged for body snatching when he was working for Wolf's father, though he certainly kept a low profile in the previous two movies. Ygor turns out to be the "long-time companion" of the monster, who lies comatose-but-alive in a tomb below the lab in which he was created, even though there was no tomb there in the previous movies. Fired with scientific zeal, Wolf revives the monster (seemed like a good idea at the time), only to find that Ygor is sending Monster out to kill the surviving members of the jury that sent him to the gallows. When Wolf is accused of the murders and the mob is howling at his gates, he kills Ygor. The monster, crazed with grief, kidnaps

Peter. Wolf and Inspector Krogh confront the monster in the lab and Monster rips off Krogh's prosthetic arm. Wolf swings across the lab on a chain and kicks Monster into a conveniently located pool of boiling sulphur (which, you guessed it, did not exist in the previous movies). Wolf basks in the gratitude of the villagers and then gets his butt out of town.

The Production

Concurrent with the Laemmles losing Universal, the British clamped down on horror movies. With the lucrative English market dead to scary pictures, Hollywood briefly gave them up. Universal began making a new kind of horror movie, ones starring Deanna Durbin. Karloff found other work easily, but Lugosi faced fifteen months of unemployment, and lost his house.

Then, in 1938, a triple feature of *Dracula*, *Frankenstein*, and *Son of Kong* unexpectedly hit a box-office jackpot. The new Universal brass (or rather, the *new* new Universal brass, as the first Laemmle replacements were already gone, drowned in a sea of red ink) saw what was happening and quickly rushed a new Frankenstein movie into production.

Colin Clive was dead. The new brass hated James Whale. So director Rowland V. Lee was given the script for *Son of Frankenstein*, a short schedule, a budget smaller than the one for *Frankenstein* eight years earlier, and told to make a sequel, quick and dirty.

Lee tossed out Willis Cooper's script and created a new story he kept in his head. The screenplay was written by Lee and Cooper as it was shot. *Son of Frankenstein* has a solidly constructed, sturdy storyline. It was clearly not improvised. But by letting the script out in only dribs and drabs as they went, the front office had no control over what Lee was doing, and contrary to their intentions, he made a first-class A-movie of much greater quality than the front office had had in mind.

Karloff was lured back to repeat his monster role one last time. Lee rejected the magnificent actor Peter Lorre for the titular son (thus unknowingly preventing the creation of what could have been the only non-comedy with Karloff and Lorre) and cast Basil Rathbone instead. The studio, knowing Lugosi's hunger for a role after his professional drought, cut his fee in half and dictated all his scenes be shot in one week. When informed of this, Lee vowed to keep Lugosi on the picture for the full production schedule, building his part way up in the process.

Added to the triumvirate of Rathbone (he receives top billing), Karloff, and Lugosi is Lionel "Pinky" Atwill, marvelously hamming his brains out as the one-armed Inspector Krogh (pronounced "crow," like the bird of death). Inspector Krogh was to become Atwill's best-remembered role.

Astonishingly, Rathbone and Atwill were both shooting *The Hound of the Baskervilles* over at 20th Century Fox *at the exact same time* that *Son of Frankenstein* was shooting at Universal.

Michael Mark and Lionel Belmore, both members of the cast of the original *Frankenstein*, were brought back to play targets of Lugosi's murderous revenge. Also on the Frankenstein town council is Gustav Von Seyffertitz, a German actor who had played Professor Moriarty opposite John Barrymore's Sherlock Holmes in a silent movie, and more recently hit a camp high as the bizarre high priest Billali in RKO's over-the-top fantasy *SHE*.

What's Good About It

Pretty much everything. It is well written, and well acted by all except the cloying child actor Donnie Dunagan as Peter von Frankenstein. Lugosi gives the best performance of his career.

Lionel Atwill tears into his role with relish, and the overacting duel between he and Rathbone is a delicious treat, top-quality scenery chewing. With almost every line each actor raises the acting stakes, getting more and more florid. It is great fun to watch, particularly when they begin playing darts. Mel Brooks didn't invent the business of sticking the darts into the inspector's wooden arm. Atwill actually does it.

The production design by Jack Otterson, though it bears no resemblance to the look of the two Whale features, is absolutely wonderful, a whole fresh gothic ambiance that really hits the evil fairy tale look on the head. The fairy tale aspect is even made explicit when the monster, described as a storybook giant by little Peter, mangles a book of fairy tales as he gets the idea to abduct the hideous child.

HAPPY BIRTHDAY, BORIS

On November 23, 1938, in the middle of shooting *Son of Frankenstein*, Boris Karloff turned fifty-one, and the cast and crew threw him a surprise birthday party. Then the news hit the set that his wife Dorothy had just given birth that very day to Boris' only child, Sarah Jane. According to the movie's publicity, Boris dashed off to the hospital to see his new daughter without removing the monster's green make-up.

Anyone familiar with *I Love Lucy* will recognize this as the plot of the episode where Ricky Ricardo dashes off to the hospital in full witch doctor make-up for the birth of Little Ricky. It seems too good a story to be true, but on the other hand, removing the monster make-up took about an hour and a half, so it may well be a genuine fact that Boris first gazed at little Sarah Jane in his full monster face.

Frank Skinner's memorable musical score was plundered for most of the subsequent Universal horrors.

Even though it is the longest of all the Universal Frankensteins, it is fast-paced with not a dull moment.

What's Bad About It

Donnie Dunagan as Peter Von Frankenstein. I shouldn't be picking on the kid, but as the movie was made in 1939, and Dunagan was born in 1934, he's over eighty years old now, so even if he sees this book, he can take it. He served honorably as a marine in Vietnam, so he's experienced far worse than a bad review in a book. He retired from acting before he was ten years old, with his last part being the title role in Walt Disney's lovely animated classic *Bambi*, a fact he kept secret from his fellow Marines. Even his wife didn't know he had been in movies and had been Bambi until she found some old memorabilia and fan letters stored in the attic.

In any event, it's a coin toss which is more grating, the little actor or the role. On meeting unbearable little Peter, Inspector Krogh explains that his right arm isn't really his arm. "Well, whose is it anyway?" asks Peter. As a Frankenstein, he naturally assumes that everyone has hand-me-down hands.

Josephine Hutchinson as Elsa von Frankenstein is no Elsa Lanchester, nor even a Valerie Hobson, but she's not terrible, and it's not her fault the part isn't very meaty. She did grow into an interesting older actress. Twenty years after playing Mrs. Frankenstein, Hutchinson played James Mason's fake wife, "Mrs. Townsend," in Hitchcock's suspense comedy *North by Northwest*.

What's Gay About It

You mean besides the entire plot hanging on the passionate love between Karloff's monster and Lugosi's Ygor? This film features the series' clearest and most unambiguous gay romance. When we stop giggling at Ygor's, "He's my friend; he—he does things for me," we have to see it as what it is: a clear statement of love. Throughout the picture, the two sacrifice for each other, kill for each other, and jealously shield each other. "He's mine! He no belong to you! You go away, not me!" Ygor snarls at Wolf Frankenstein in a jealous rage over the monster.

When Wolf decides to repair his malfunctioning half-brother, Wolf alters the mean-spirited graffiti someone has scrawled on his father's tomb, "Maker of Monsters," so it now reads "Heinrich Von Frankenstein, Maker of Men."

Elsa babbles to Inspector Krogh about Wolf's new experiments over breakfast. "He's terribly preoccupied now," she blathers to the policeman investigating her husband, adding, "but just as soon as his problem's solved, he'll be gay as a lark again. He's like that." Elsa hasn't a shred of discretion, but she's a very liberal wife.

Regarding the sulphur pit, Wolf tells Elsa, "Our family history states that the structure was built by the Romans over a natural sulphur pit, and used by them as mineral baths." Actually, his "family history," that is, the two previous movies, had the monster built in a watchtower a few miles out of town, not over a Roman sulphur pit in the Frankenstein back yard. But if we take it as true, then the monster being gay makes even more sense; he was made in a bathhouse.

The scene where the monster, now ambulatory at last, first meets his little brother, is a great one. Sighting himself in a large mirror, the monster carries on like a runway model who has just discovered he has a zit on his nose. He drags Wolf over to the mirror and compares their faces, clearly feeling that their dad gave him the fuzzy end of the lollipop. Fortunately, Ygor shows up, turns the mirror away, and calms his lover down by stroking his massive pecs. All the monster ever wanted was love, and now he has it from a grotesque, homicidal fiend.

When Wolf says the monster isn't well yet mentally, still being gay and all, Ygor's ferociously jealous side surfaces. "He's well enough for me, and you no touch him again!"

"Oh," replies Wolf, seeing how things are, but unable to state it plainly in 1939. In trying to describe it to his butler, Benson, Wolf says the monster is, "Dangerous of course, but he loves Ygor and obeys him." There it is. Out and proud.

Wolf finds Ygor and the monster cuddling and caressing on the operating table. I'm not kidding. It's clearly afterglow from the murders which so often stand in for sex in these movies.

SIBLING RIVALRY 97

When Wolf tries putting his own hand gently on Monster's torso, Monster growls, grossed out by the attempted incest, and Ygor snatches Wolf's hand away. Ygor's look of seething jealousy needs no dialogue to explain, and gets none. It's there on the screen for the world to see.

The climax erupts from the monster's howling grief and rage when he discovers his lover's murder in what is a very moving scene of gay bereavement. Camp is gone. Karloff's howl as he cradles Ygor's body tears at your heart. After gently laying out Ygor's body in the tomb, the monster predictably runs amok, destroying the lab and then kidnapping Peter.

Eventually, Krogh gets his fake arm torn off again, Rathbone's stunt double swings across the lab on a chain like an urbane, overdressed Tarzan, kicking Karloff's stunt double into the sulphur pit, and Wolf reaffirms his heterosexual identity by saving his horrid child, re-embracing his wife, and leaving perverted Transylvania, or wherever the hell they are, to return to the good ol' USA, land of normalcy.

Aftermath

Basil Rathbone, happy to take the money and the billing, was otherwise dismissive of the picture. He omits any reference to *Son of Frankenstein* from his wildly egotistical autobiography, *In and Out of Character*. (It's quite a read. His ego screams from the pages.) Rathbone certainly liked to dominate a set, and regale all and sundry with stories, but his warmth was elusive. In his later years he would refuse autographs for young fans if they presented him with monster magazines with his photos on the covers to sign, as attested to by author Mark Thomas McGee in his book *Fast and Furious: The Story of American-International Pictures*, to whom this happened when he was a teenager.

Unbelievably, *Son of Frankenstein* premiered at the Pantages Theater in Hollywood a mere *eight days* after it completed shooting. Given its never-finished script, the way it ran over-schedule and over-budget, and the most rushed post-production period I've ever heard of, it's amazing the picture isn't a terrible mess, but it isn't. From here on in, the front office's determination to make cheap little B-pictures of its monsters would prevail.

WHERE THERE'S AN ATWILL, THERE'S A FAY WRAY

I confess to a tremendous fondness for Lionel "Pinky" Atwill, Hollywood's maddest scientist. Pinky made a whole string of horror thrillers of his own, including *Doctor X* and *The Mystery of the Wax Museum*, both two-color Technicolor shockers with *King Kong*'s Fay Wray, the latter film remade in the 1950s with Vincent Price. Pinky also played the title role in *The Mad Doctor of Market Street*. Although he was kindly Dr. Mortimer in Rathbone's first outing as Sherlock Holmes, *The Hound of the Baskervilles*, he was fated to become Rathbone's evil nemesis Professor Moriarty in *Sherlock Holmes and the Secret Weapon*. The list of villains and mad doctors he played is lengthy indeed, and his fun Inspector Krogh was his first of five appearances in Frankenstein movies.

But Lionel was his own worst enemy. "Women are cat creatures," he foolishly purred in a 1933 interview. "Their preference is for a soft fireside cushion, for delicate bowls of cream, for perfumed leisure, *and for a master*," hinting at what turned out to be a very real libertine side to him. Pinky was given to throwing weekend orgies at his palatial home, full of group sex, cross-dressing, porn movies shown and made, some witnesses say *directed by Atwill himself*, and it became his sad downfall.

Pinky was convicted of perjury in 1942 for having denied under oath a Yuletide orgy he'd thrown in his home that involved re-enacting porn movies with, unfortunately for Pinky, at least one loose-lipped young woman with a penchant for sexual blackmail. He was also convicted of "owning lewd films." Yes, he went to jail in part for owning porn movies. It was a different California back then.

The moralistic prigs of the Breen Office declared Pinky unemployable, but Universal courageously kept him working in defiance of the blue-nosed blacklist, casting him in small roles in several films during the tragically short interval between his disgrace and his death from cancer in 1946 at the age of sixty-one. His stylish cinematic evil lives on in immortal movies, and who doesn't possess a "lewd" film or two these days? I may have one or two or a hundred myself.

And really, aren't women cat creatures? We all know men are dogs.

14

PROFANING HIS NAME: THE *FRANKENSTEIN* B-MOVIE SEQUELS

The Ghost of Frankenstein (1942)
Frankenstein Meets the Wolfman (1943)
House of Frankenstein (1944)
House of Dracula (1945)

(Just the Frankenstein Monster bits)

You would-be Frankenstein!
— Jailor (Charles Wagonhelm) to Dr. Gustav Niemann

Don't profane his name with your dirty lips.
— Gustav Niemann (Boris Karloff),
expressing respect in *House of Frankenstein*

Remember *The Montagues*, Shakespeare's sequel to *Romeo & Juliet*, where those two nutty teenagers wake back up and have more adventures on their way to being united forever? No? Maybe that's because Shakespeare forgot to write it in his hurry to get *Pericles*, *Cymbaline*, and *Timon of Athens* into theaters in time for the Tony Awards. But those other two star-crossed lovers, the Frankenstein Monster and Ygor, did get a second shot at love, this time to be so deeply united, no man could ever tear them asunder again.

By 1942, the latest Universal regime was reaping good money by making B-movie monster films, and it was

Frankenstein's turn. Although Sir Cedric Hardwicke was to play Ludwig Frankenstein, Henry and Elizabeth's younger son, they titled it *The Ghost of Frankenstein*, probably because calling it "Yet Another Son of Frankenstein" sounded lame.

Bela Lugosi, who only three years earlier had lost his house, had just bought a new one he liked much better. Now, not only was he returning to his best role, but Boris Karloff was 3000 miles away, starring on Broadway in *Arsenic and Old Lace*.

With Karloff unavailable and the Universal bosses unimpressed with Lugosi's, ah, versatility, they decided to create a new horror star, and they went with Creighton Chaney, firmly rechristened Lon Chaney Jr. Brilliant as Lenny in *Of Mice and Men*, effective and even touching as Larry Talbot, he was considerably less winning in other roles.

And then there was the alcohol problem. People passing by the soundstages where *Ghost of Frankenstein* was shooting often saw the weird spectacle of the Frankenstein Monster slipping out the door for a quick belt from his hip flask. As the afternoons wore on, the monster became unsteady in his giant shoes.

Dr. Frankenstein must have been very good at curing death. Not only are the monster and Ygor still alive, but Michael Mark and Lionel Belmore, who both also died in *Son of Frankenstein*, are alive and well, and even Dwight Frye, who had died in both *Frankenstein* and in *Bride of Frankenstein*, was also still around, and he survives this time.

The discontented villagers basically apply for a mob permit, this being a town with a long, proud history of torch-bearing lynch mobs. The mayor gives the mob permission to blow up Castle Frankenstein. This seems like an awfully lax way to govern. Blowing up the castle uncovers the monster who, like every other dead person in the district, is still alive.

Well, let's say still ambulatory. As played by Lon Chaney Jr., though he is huge (Chaney was a much larger man than Karloff), he shows little life. Only a single stony expression sits on his face, and he never emits so much as a grunt or a growl.

The amiably silly plot has Ygor guiding his re-resurrected lover to the mythical village of Visaria, where dwells Henry Frankenstein's previously unmentioned other son, Ludwig.

Ludwig is played by Sir Cedric Hardwicke. George Bernard Shaw once told Hardwicke, "You are my fifth favorite actor, the other four being the Marx Brothers." Hardwicke was flattered by this, despite the fact that it classifies him as a lesser actor than Zeppo Marx. Cedric is solid, and as always, his voice is honey, but his performance is colorless and dull.

When we meet Ludwig, he and his associates, saintly Dr. Kettering and mad fiend Dr. Bohmer (did Ludwig hire them to balance each other?), have just removed a man's brain, operated on it, and then replaced it again. I would not volunteer for this operation. I suspect that while the patient's brain was absent, that his brainless body wrote this movie.

Lionel Atwill plays disgraced Dr. Bohmer, who committed some unfortunate surgical transgression years before that ruined his career. "In those days, I was the master, Frankenstein was just the pupil, but…I made a slight *miscalculation*," he says bitterly in the patented Atwill mad scientist fashion. We never learn just what his *miscalculation* was, but given Atwill's delivery of the line, I doubt it was in the bill.

Also in Visaria is Ludwig's daughter, Elsa, I assume named after the monster bride. There is not the slightest mention by anyone of Elsa's mother. One suspects that Ludwig tinkered Elsa together in the lab in a hot three-way with Kettering and Bohmer. Elsa is played by lovely Evelyn Ankers. While brains are being transplanted all around her, she wants one of town prosecutor Erik Ernst's (played by Ralph Bellamy) organs put inside her. Bellamy gets to play a courtroom scene, where he has to cross-examine the Frankenstein Monster with a straight face. You try it.

When the monster meets Ludwig in court, the monster recognizes him. I'll be damned if I can figure out when and where they met before.

Ygor has noticed what a one-note performance Chaney is giving and wants the monster's former vitality restored by Ludwig. "Pour life into his hungry veins," says Ygor to Ludwig, accidentally reverting to Dracula imagery.

So what should Ludwig do with his big brother? Common sense says dismantle him. Tree-hugging liberals like me would say teach him to sing "Puttin' on the Ritz," and then he and

Ygor can get an apartment together in West Visaria. The Hippocratic Oath says cure him. And the ghost of Henry Frankenstein, who conveniently shows up looking and sounding like Hardwicke in a different wig, suggests a brain transplant. Ludwig listens to Daddy.

Ludwig wants to use the brain of saintly murdered Dr. Kettering. Pathologically jealous Ygor has a hissy fit at the mention of this. Gay passion rings out as he shouts, "No, no, no! You can not take my friend away from me! He's all I have, nothing else. You're going to make him your friend and I will be alone!" Ygor wants his own, not-at-all-saintly brain put in the monster.

The monster has his own agenda regarding whose brain he'd like to have installed in his square skull. In a very clear statement of his previously unsuspected transgender tendencies, the monster makes it abundantly clear that he wants the brain of Little Chloe, a very small *girl*, placed in his skull. To my amazement, the monster is a bottom.

It's really a shame they don't take up the monster's plan. The Frankenstein Monster with the developing brain of a little girl, and a little girl with the monster's violent criminal brain, now *that* would have made a fascinating movie. *Myra Breckenstein*. (A few years ago, I met Janet Ann Gallow, who played Little Chloe, and I made her giggle when I said how I thought her then-very-small brain would have rattled around in the monster's roomy head.)

Ygor wins the brain donor pool by conning Bohmer into pulling a switcheroo. Brilliant Dr. Bohmer gets conned by an illiterate, half-crazed shepherd and makes another slight miscalculation.

Guess what? It all goes terribly wrong. Didn't see that coming, did you? Bohmer neglects to check Ygor's and the monster's blood types. Oops. The monster wakes up with Ygor's voice, but blind. Of course, the mismatched blood types would actually just kill him outright, but there seems little point in complaining about one small medical error in a movie full of *brain transplants*. Anyway, Bohmer, Ludwig, and Monster-Ygor all die in the spectacular conflagration while Chloe is returned to her father, and Elsa and Erik escape the rampaging mob that naturally shows up, albeit too late to accomplish anything.

It's a silly mess of a movie, but it's short, it's never boring, and the music is good. Ygor and the monster, horror's Romeo and Juliet, now forever united in one body, may be dead, but if this film has said anything at all, it's that no one's deaths in these movies ever lasts longer than it takes to mount a sequel, and the sequel to this one lay only fifty-one weeks away.

Frankenstein Meets the Wolfman is not really a dreadful movie. It's vastly better than either of the "House of" pictures. Yes, it spirals downhill quite quickly once Bela Lugosi shows up as the monster, but up until then, it's not bad.

Curt Siodmak, author of the novel *Donovan's Brain*, wrote the movie. He claimed it began as a joke title he came up with, *Frankenstein Wolfs the Meat Man*, and someone took him up on it.

Lon Chaney was supposed to play both the monster and the Wolfman, like a horror version of Peter Sellers, but after they realized what that would cost in special effects, not to mention that having an actor who was usually too drunk to work after lunch playing both leads would slow production to a crawl, they thought better of it, and Lon lucked out by getting to play Lawrence Talbot, doing most of the role in his natural face.

But someone had to play the monster. A person who got paid to make this decision remembered that Ygor's brain had been put into the monster's head in the last movie, so why not cast Bela Lugosi? It's possibly Bela's worst-ever performance.

But is it really Bela's fault? In *Frankenstein Meets the Wolfman*, Lugosi is sixty years old, addicted to drugs, terribly frail, and in no physical shape even to submit to the make-up and heavy costume, let alone lug Ilona Massey around in his arms, or wrestle with Chaney's stunt double. Most of the time you're actually watching Eddie Parker play the monster, with Bela Lugosi pretty much confined to ruining close-ups.

Lugosi apologists are quick to point out that Lugosi's dialogue scenes, which established that the monster spoke and was blind, were cut before release, thus making his staggering stiff-armed around the set, in the rare shots when it's actually Bela doing the staggering, look ridiculous. That might fly except that even when one does know he's supposed to be blind, he still looks ridiculous.

Why was all the monster's dialogue cut? Because it made preview audiences howl with laughter. Curt Siodmak placed the blame squarely on Lugosi. Curt was even more disdainful of Bela's talent than I am. He actually said, "Bela couldn't act his way out of a paper bag." I believe that with a good script and a strong director, Bela *could* act his way out of a paper bag.

While there is no doubt that the Frankenstein Monster giving long speeches in Bela Lugosi's voice would be pretty silly (it was pretty silly in the final scenes of *Ghost of Frankenstein*), I've read the scenes. I don't think Laurence Olivier could have played those scenes in that make-up without getting laughs. I'm afraid Siodmak must share the blame. In the words of Boris Karloff, "Poor Bela."

Bela's unfortunate performance is only further highlighted by Chaney being really good in the movie. Talbot is smack-dab center in his acting comfort zone, and he gives one of his best-ever performances.

In this film, an accidentally resurrected Larry Talbot travels around Europe seeking "release" (sounds like Saturday night in West Hollywood), accompanied by his chaperone, the old gypsy crone Maleva, played by the terminally camp Maria Ouspenskaya. They travel to good old Visaria, hoping that Ludwig Frankenstein can either cure or kill Larry Talbot.

Dwight Frye, at the end of his career and nearly at the end of his life, is again a hothead in the mob, but in a new town. He apparently moved *from* Frankenstein *to* Visaria. How bad is his real estate agent?

Lionel Atwill is the nameless mayor, I assume because no one even creepier was available. Elsa Frankenstein is now Ilona Massey, a refugee from MGM musicals, who was probably in Universal's Visaria trying to hide from Nelson Eddy. (The laugh is on her. Nelson was on the Universal lot also, making *The Phantom of the Opera*, and in color.) There's no sign of Ralph Bellamy, but his absence isn't nearly as puzzling as where Elsa got the thick German accent she didn't have in the previous movie. We are told she is the last of the Frankensteins, which means annoying little Peter von Frankenstein must be dead along with his parents. Did they sail back to America on the *Titanic*?

Patric Knowles, a terrifically gorgeous actor who later achieved gay immortality as Lindsey Woolsey, the final husband of Mame Dennis in the camp classic film *Auntie Mame*, plays Dr. Mannering, the Wolfman's personal physician.

Larry finds the monster frozen in ice. Bela's prominent nose and dimpled chin are so conspicuously displayed in the monster make-up that when the monster is Eddie Parker, as he is in the ice, you can't miss it. I guess the "stunt" of just sitting there was too much for Bela.

One treat in this film for Broadway queens is the series' only musical number, "Faro La Faro Li," sung by a big cheesy gypsy character, played by an actual gypsy named Adia Kuznetzoff. Adia had played a heavy comic foil opposite Laurel & Hardy in one of their lesser Roach features, *Swiss Miss*.

The song is performed at the Festival of the New Wine, a sort of monster's pride festival in celebration of public drunkenness held in Visaria. A couple hundred extras cavort about in Tyrolean drag while Adia bellows Siodmak's gay lyrics:

> They'll be no music in the tomb,
> So sing, rejoice, and down with gloom,
> Tonight the new wine is in bloom,
> Faro, faro, faro lo.

I'm sorry. I don't drink. Does wine "bloom"?

As if that wasn't morbid and cheesy enough, Adia makes the mistake of addressing a verse directly to Elsa and Larry:

> To them I toast come drink with me,
> And may they happy ever be,
> And may they live *eternally*,
> Faro, faro, faro la.
> Come one and all and sing a song,
> Faro la, faro li,
> For life is short, but death is *long*,
> Faro La, faro li.

Talbot has been eyeing the exits all through the aggressively jolly song. Being threatened with eternal life when he's all about his death wish causes him to freak out and make a scene. (Scene 23.)

When the monster crashes the party, everybody screams and runs around, although without his seeing-eye werewolf, the blind monster is fairly harmless. The peasants have to keep screaming so the monster will know where to chase them.

Dr. Mannering quickly discovers what his predecessors did, that merging male monsters is more interesting than boring a boring girlfriend. Instead of dismantling the monster, he naturally decides to power him up, even though a full moon is rising.

Just as the monster is fully revived, Talbot transforms into his macho bear of an alter-ego, and it's just too many queens for one spotlight, so a major bitch-slap brawl ensues. Eddie Parker now doubles Chaney, so another stunt man, Gil Perkins, doubles the monster for the fight of whatever century this is supposed to be. (All the Universal monster movies are vague, to put it mildly, about when they take place.) Since Perkins looks nothing like Lugosi nor Parker, the monster has three easily distinguished faces in this movie. Chaney and Lugosi handled some close-ups, but otherwise sat on the sidelines, Lugosi enjoying a cigar while Chaney got drunk as Parker and Perkins played their roles for them, until interrupted by the usual killjoy village guardians of morality blowing up a dam that wasn't there in the last movie.

All the monsters are washed away while Elsa and Dr. Mannering, who have learned their lesson about the hazards of abnormal sex, go off together, looking for a musical to be in. By the ridiculous ending, it was hard to believe the series could ever sink any lower, but it promptly did.

We rejoin *House of Frankenstein*, already in progress. The Lampini House of Horrors arrives at the village of Frankenstein, where we find the ruins of Castle Frankenstein and its burst dam, which is odd, since the dam was in Visaria, not Frankenstein.

Production on *House of Frankenstein* began only a month after *Frankenstein Meets the Wolfman* was released. The script was written *before* the previous movie was in theaters. Lon Chaney and Lionel Atwill are in both films. They were both photographed by the same man, scored by the same men, and for Heaven's sake, Curt "Brain Transplants" Siodmak wrote both of them. How can it be that *no one* noticed that they had the towns wrong?

PROFANING HIS NAME

Gustav Niemann and Daniel, looking for those infamous Frankenstein records, accidentally find Larry Talbot and the Frankenstein Monster, frozen in a subterranean ice chamber. Naturally, they thaw them out and set them free. Wouldn't you?

Once having acquired Frankenstein's notebooks, Gustav, Daniel the hunchback, the Wolfman, the monster, and Ilonka, a gypsy dancing girl also procured during their character shopping spree in Frankenstein, are off to Visaria, although that's really where they just were.

At Visaria, Gustav finds his old castle, dirty but intact. (*Every* scientist on earth has a castle. You should see Stephen Hawking's.) There actually is a cleaning-the-castle montage. One half-expects Ilonka to invite in forest animals (wolves, bats, etc.) to help clean while singing "Whistle While You Work."

Revenge-mad Gustav now collects his old enemies, Strauss, played by Michael Mark, and Ullman, played by *King Kong*'s Frank Reicher, preparatory to playing a complex game of musical brains.

"I'm going to give that brain of yours a new home, in the skull of the Frankenstein Monster," Gustav snarls menacingly to Ullman, who appears inexplicably afraid of being removed from his aging *mortal* body, to be placed in a big, strong *immortal* body. It evidentially never occurs to Gustav that putting your enemy's brain into the body of a super-strong, uncontrollable, immortal monster is just buying yourself more trouble.

Gustav threatens little Strauss with putting Talbot's lycanthropic brain into his head. Wouldn't this just mean that Talbot would still be alive and whining to die, only in a wimpier body?

Gustav and Daniel remove Ullman's and Stauss' brains and pop them into jars for later transplanting, not unlike my Aunt Mary preserving nectarines. What is the shelf life of bottled brains?

In a curiously homo-erotic plot development even for a Frankenstein film, Daniel decides he wants Talbot's body—literally. Daniel wants to be inside Talbot, albeit cranially. Gustav refuses to comply, as I'm sure would Talbot if asked. Gustav says, "Talbot's body is the perfect home for the monster's brain." I think he should give serious consideration just to discarding the monster's brain, which used to be Ygor's brain, and was never very pleasant at the best of times.

Ilonka comes in and has a spat with Daniel, diplomatically telling him, "I hate you! You're mean and you're ugly. I hate you! I hate you! I hate you!" Ilonka, played by 19-year-old Elena Verdugo, later a regular on the TV program *Marcus Welby, MD*, shot at the same studio, displays all the emotional maturity of a girl her age (and leaves out that Daniel is also a murderer).

In a fit of jealousy, little Daniel, the love-sick hunchback, plays some rough S&M games, vigorously lashing the strapped-down monster with a leather strap, an ill-advised form of recreation. Whipping the Frankenstein Monster is *not* safe sex. Daniel will live to regret it, but not for long.

Up to this point, the Frankenstein Monster, now played by the aptly named Glenn Strange, has lain in the ice, lain in the show wagon, and lain on the operating table.

The Village of Visaria Municipal Volunteer Torch-Bearing Mob shows up on cue. Are these "Save the Children" homophobes? Well, one of them actually says, "Our children aren't safe," as they rouse themselves into a movie-ending fury.

The Wolfman kills Ilonka, who returns the favor. (More on that later in this book.) Grief-stricken Daniel blames Gustav for the death of this woman who was killed by Talbot, and attacks Gustav. This enrages the freshly recharged Frankenstein Monster, who is still sore, in every sense, over Daniel's whipping game. The monster, and all Hell, break loose. Daniel gets defenestrated. (It only sounds dirty.) The good news is that the monster's blindness has cleared up. Aren't you happy for him?

The monster defends his new boy friend, Dr. Niemann, from the mob, so they use their torches to drive him into a conveniently located nearby swamp, dragging Gustav with him. It's almost kind of romantic, except for seeing fifty-seven-year-old Karloff doing his own head-going-under-the-quicksand shot. What a pro. One can see why he was so overjoyed to escape from Universal to Val Lewton's smarter films over at RKO. But for the poor old monster, a further indignity remained, a movie without even "Frankenstein" in the title.

PROFANING HIS NAME

Twenty minutes or so into *House of Dracula*, Dr. Edelmann and Larry Talbot find a dried mud flow with the Frankenstein Monster and the skeleton of Dr. Niemann poking out, in a cave beneath the clinic where Edelmann is treating Dracula and the Wolfman. *What a coincidence!* How much time has passed since *House of Frankenstein*? Well, that skeleton hints that it's been a long time. Everything else makes it look like about a week, and cleaned-up, nattily mustachioed Larry Talbot actually looks younger than he did in the previous movie.

They take the monster up some stairs to the lab, although just leaving him in the mud seems a smarter option. Edelmann says that these stairs were to "the old torture chamber." Don't you wish your doctor had an old torture chamber under his or her clinic?

Since the monster is comatose *yet again*, Edelmann starts reviving him, like you do, because killing him "would be murder." Of course, reviving him would be murders. Nina, Edelmann's hunchatrix helper, and Larry Talbot talk him out of it, so the monster is just left lying on the giant operating table that Edelmann just happens to have, while the ambulatory characters wander off into other plotlines. The idea that the monster can be a character, in fact a compelling character, himself, doesn't seem to have occurred to anyone working on this movie.

It is another twenty minutes before the movie remembers it has the Frankenstein Monster just lying around like a prop, and sends the nutty monster version of Dr. Edelmann to the lab to charge him up, in hopes that the monster can join the story. The local torch-bearing mob is already en route, wanting this pervert clinic shut down, when Nina checks on the noise in the lab and discovers the monster actually moving very slightly.

Nutty Edelmann is blathering about making him stronger than he's ever been, and giving him "the strength of a hundred men." Doesn't seem a good idea. And given how little he has to do in this movie, I think the strength of ten men really would have sufficed. As he says this, he is patting and caressing the monster. Nice as it is to see the monster getting a little man-love, his first since Ygor's brain was put in his skull (you can't count his multi-year submerged mud-cuddle with Gustav Niemann; it wasn't reciprocal), I can't help noticing that the monster is being shot full of electricity, and touching him should electrocute Edelmann.

Although the monster is now strongly considering rousing himself up off the table someday soon, Edelmann nonetheless handles Nina's murder himself. Great. Now the monster is just *watching* murders. Good thing he got his eyesight back or he'd have nothing at all to do.

Edelmann's other assistant, Miliza, along with Larry Talbot, Police Inspector Holtz (played by Lionel Atwill), and an anonymous extra cop all barge in just in time to see Nina die, and the monster decides to join in the fun, in defense of his latest boyfriend, Nutty Edelmann. Guess who the monster kills first. If you guessed the nameless extra cop, award yourself ten points. However, just seconds later the monster hurls Holtz into an electrical apparatus that kills him in a shower of sparks, exactly the same way he killed Atwill back in *Ghost of Frankenstein*. Old habits are hard to break.

Talbot shoots Edelmann while the monster just watches passively, but once Edelmann is dead, the monster gets pissed and comes for Talbot, whom he has fought before, back on their first date. Talbot knocks over some free-standing shelves in the center of the room and a conflagration instantly flares up. You know, if you have a lot of beakers which, if broken, will instantly ignite a fire so hot it will burn down a room made of stone, perhaps you shouldn't store them on flimsy, free-standing shelves in the center of the room. The cat could knock it over. What? They couldn't afford a lever that blows up the clinic?

The monster flails about in footage economically lifted from the fiery climax of *Ghost of Frankenstein*, which includes close-ups of Chaney as the monster and long shots of Eddie Parker, also as the monster. That is four different men, Strange, Karloff (in flashbacks lifted from *Bride of Frankenstein*), Chaney, and Parker, all seen playing the monster in a movie in which the grand total of screen time he has doing anything other than lying on a table or in a heap of mud is less than three minutes. One wonders how Fred Gwynne got left out.

You know who I blame for this great, immortal character being reduced to an ineffectual bogeyman who only lumbers about in a movie's last two minutes? Boris Karloff. While making *Bride of Frankenstein*, he bitched and moaned about the monster ceasing to be a mute character and learning to speak, and he continued to bitch about it for the rest of his life.

James Whale, gay genius, realized that in *Frankenstein*, the monster was a newborn infant, but that in *Bride of Frankenstein*, he was a learning and developing adolescent. If this perfectly logical and sensible arc had been continued, by *Son of Frankenstein* the monster could have been an adult, albeit a very maladjusted one, speaking and thinking in a more sophisticated manner, and developing into an increasingly interesting character. It happens in the book.

But Karloff, straight actor, was in love with his original interpretation, and just wanted to repeat it. It's a rare instance of a good actor objecting to his character developing and deepening. His endless complaining about the monster speaking got Rowland V. Lee to restore the monster's muteness in *Son of Frankenstein* just to keep Boris happy. The result was that, instead of developing, the monster had regressed into a creative dead end. As long as the monster couldn't develop past a mute, uncomprehending infant, he *was* played out. When making him talk like Ygor turned out to be a disaster, the role was dead. It wasn't beauty that killed this beast. Karloff murdered his own monster. Great actor, but there's a reason he never wrote nor directed.

The Frankenstein Monster had one more play date on his calendar, with guys named Bud and Lou.

15

ALL'S WELLS THAT ENDS WELLS
Two Very Mad Scientists from H.G. Wells

Unlike Jules Verne, the younger H.G. Wells lived to see several of his books and stories find their way to the screen. He even wrote the screenplays for the two of them: *The Man Who Could Work Miracles* and *Things to Come*. (The little-known comic fantasy *The Man Who Could Work Miracles*, which is outside the subject matter of this book, is a complete delight. If you've never seen it, or even if you have, allow me to recommend it. And Ernest Thesiger is in it.)

Most of Wells' scientists were, at worst, loveably eccentric, like Professor Cavor in *The First Men in the Moon*, played memorably and delightfully in a movie by the wonderful British comic actor Lionel Jeffries, and more recently on British TV equally delightfully by the also wonderful British comic actor-writer (in fact, he wrote the Wells TV movie he appeared in) Mark Gatiss. However, perhaps Wells' two maddest, most malevolent scientists, Doctors Griffin and Moreau, both found their way to the screen in the early 1930s, in Universal's *The Invisible Man* and Paramount's *Island of Lost Souls*. Moreau made monsters; Griffin became one.

16

HERE'S LOOKING AT YOU, KID
The Invisible Man (1933)

> *Even the moon is frightened of me, frightened to death. The whole world is frightened to death.*
> — Dr. Jack Griffin (Claude Rains), being very full of himself

The Story

A rustic inn in the English village of Iping is visited during a howling winter snowstorm by a mysterious and ill-tempered man who wears bandages covering all of his face except for his protruding nose. The man rents a room, demanding absolute privacy. As the weeks pass, he grows more irritable and rude, even assaulting the landlord. When the local constable comes to evict him, the stranger strips naked and even hurls his fake nose at them, but his clothes seem to hold no person.

He is Dr. Jack Griffin, and in self-experimentation has turned himself invisible, and is now desperate to discover a way to become visible again. Unbeknownst to him, one of the invisibility ingredients, monocaine, causes paranoid insanity, and Griffin is losing his mind.

Griffin enlists the aid of a co-worker, Dr. Kemp, to return to Iping to retrieve his research logs. While there, Griffin kills a police captain in full invisible view of the assembled townspeople, establishing the reality of a rampaging, homicidal invisible man.

Nationwide panic ensues, while Griffin goes on a power-mad killing spree, attacking strangers, robbing banks (only to throw the cash in the streets for passersby to pocket—a socialist Invisible Man?), and wrecking a train. When Dr. Kemp betrays him to the authorities, Griffin vows vengeance on him. Easily slipping past the elaborate police guards, Griffin sends Kemp off a cliff in a car. Eventually taking refuge in a barn, Griffin falls asleep. The farmer hears him snoring and reports to the police that "there's breathing in my barn." The cops surround the barn and set fire to it. (Shades of the villagers and the old mill in *Frankenstein*, though this time it's lawful authority, not a torch-bearing mob, committing murder-by-arson.) When the barn door opens, the police open fire at the approaching footprints, and the shape of a body is pressed into the snow. Later in the hospital, as Griffin dies, he regains visibility, and the movie-going public gets its first look at Claude Rains.

The Production

When James Whale was in pre-production for *The Invisible Man* in 1933, Karloff was set to star, but he and Universal couldn't reach an agreement on money, so Karloff ankled. Colin Clive was choice number two, but he was anxious to return to England. Actually, he was just generally anxious. Whale knew Claude Rains from the London theater and knew that Rains' amazing voice was just what his invisible man needed.

Griffin is given a female love interest, in the person of beautiful Gloria Stuart, that same woman you want to strangle when she drops the diamond into the ocean in *Titanic*. She plays Griffin's fiancée Flora, whom Whale often photographs surrounded by flowers, in case we have forgotten what her name means. In the book, Griffin has no girlfriend. Wells' Griffin may very well be gay. Wells' character in the novel is also an albino, giving him additional motivation to want to be invisible.

Wells' character of Kemp is made into a romantic rival for Griffin, modeled on the Henry-Elizabeth-Victor triangle in *Frankenstein*, only Kemp is seen immediately as a sniveling worm, bad-mouthing Griffin behind his back to Flora well before he learns Jack has become a homicidal maniac, and later on, Kemp is revealed as a craven coward. He says of Griffin, "He meddled in things men should leave alone." Needless to say, this line was never written by the atheist Wells. And Kemp is meddling with a girl he should leave alone as he says it.

What's Good About It

Absolutely everything. It's a masterpiece. Often thought of as a special-effects movie, it's a rare example of an effects-heavy film where you come away thinking about its vivid characters, the compelling story, the wonderful humor, the great acting, and the striking dialogue, rather than the effects. Mind you, the effects are *amazing* for 1933 (the same year as *King Kong*), but it's a great movie overall. It's always entertaining, whether stuff is floating about on wires, or empty pants are running about singing, or hilarious Una O'Conner is just sneaking a drink or screeching. And, like the classic semi-satirical novel it's based on, it's often very funny.

Rains' voice is thrilling honey as he speaks the great, literate verbal arias written for him by R.C. Sherriff and (uncredited) Preston Sturgis and Phillip Wylie. (Sturgis, of course, became one of the greatest comedy writer-directors ever, while Wylie was one of my favorite book authors, who gave us, among others, the amazing science-fiction novel *The Disappearance* and the non-fiction book-length essay *A Generation of Vipers*—the latter book heavily influenced the development of my thinking—as well as co-authoring the novels *When Worlds Collide* and *After Worlds Collide*.) "The drugs I took seemed to light up my brain. Suddenly I realized the power I held; the power to rule, to make the world grovel at my feet." Later, to Flora, his megalomania rises to even greater, more absurd heights, "Even the moon's frightened of me, frightened to death. The whole world is frightened to death!"

Rains' vocal performance is great. He takes himself through vocal pyrotechnics he never again indulged in when he could be seen. He's not afraid to scream, to cackle, to run riot. His sudden outbreaks of violence are so unpredictable, so driven by a deep, mad rage, and contrast so vividly with the gentle comedy around them, that they are genuinely disturbing, even when viewed today, more than eighty years later.

What's Bad About It

Once again, Whale turns out a film without any flaws. Oh, all right. Henry Travers' performance as Flora's father, the stodgy old scientist Griffin and Kemp work for, is a bit dull, but then, stodgy and dull was his specialty (Hitchcock used him very well indeed in his masterful *Shadow of a Doubt* a decade later), and William Harrigan does not exactly light up the screen as Kemp, though he's convincingly slimy and craven. Are you happy now?

What's Gay About It

James Whale made this movie, a man who never put anything *unintentionally* gay into a movie. The first clear line of dialogue is, "Did you hear about Mrs. Mason's little Willy?" Having a little willy is enough to make any man wish they were invisible at times; think how much worse it must be for a woman to have one. Clearly, hers is provoking gossip.

Given that, in movies of the 1930s, gays were the invisible people, there but never to be seen nor mentioned, and given how Jack Griffin spends the movie cut off from mankind, a stranger even among his friends, desperately trying to find a way to fit back into humanity, and when that fails, seeking revenge against the human race, and given that he spends a lot of time running around stark naked, often outside, even in crowds of people, I see some gay identification there. At least he's not obsessed with his looks.

And for the horror angle, he's the most-sinister homo of all. He's *invisible*! He's not an obvious, effeminate queen; he's *undetectable*. He could be standing behind you, looking at your butt while you shower. He could be teaching your kids *drama*!

Aftermath

The success of *The Invisible Man* spawned a string of sequels.

The Invisible Man Returns (1940), written by Curt Siodmak, is deceptively titled, as Jack Griffin is dead. Vincent Price plays his first horror lead as the Invisible Man, another mellifluous voice. But this time he isn't even a mad doctor. He's a man framed by Sir Cedric Hardwicke for murder. His friend, Dr. Frank Griffin, Jack Griffin's previously unmentioned brother, gives Price a shot of his brother's invisibility drug, which he happens to have lying around, to escape from prison and expose the real killer. Price is a good guy who kills nobody. The only suspense is: will the drug drive him mad before he clears himself? At the end he is cured and lives happily ever after with his girlfriend. The movie is a heavy-handed B, and despite Vincent Price and some even-better special effects, doesn't compare at all with Whale's superb film.

The Invisible Woman (not to be confused with the 2014 Ralph Fiennes-directed movie *The Invisible Woman*, which is a docudrama about Charles Dickens' affair with the actress Ellen Tiernan, the titular "invisible" woman) was also released in 1940, and also written by Siodmak. There is no real connection to Wells' novel at all. John Barrymore's Professor Gibbs isn't mad, just eccentric enough for a Thorne Smith novel. (Smith was the author of such fantasy-based comedy novels as *Topper*, *Turnabout*, and *Nightlife of the Gods*. He's one of my favorite novelists, and if you've never read one of his books, I strongly recommend you do. They are hilarious, and have been the basis for a number of wonderful movies.)

This must be the only American movie of its era to have a naked woman cavorting throughout the picture, but don't get too excited; she's invisible. Belovedly hatchet-faced Margaret Hamilton is left visible, to engage in broad comic banter with Barrymore in this out-and-out slapstick comedy. Where else can you see the magic chemistry of the most unlikely screen pairing of all-time: John Barrymore and Shemp Howard?

Invisible Agent (1942), which is not about an actor's representative who never shows up for meetings or takes his clients' calls, but rather is a science-fiction World War II espionage thriller, again finds Siodmak penning the script. He was apparently as much the go-to scenarist for invisibility as he was the bard of brain transplants. Dr. Frank Griffin (Jon Hall), grandson of Jack Griffin, who died unmarried and childless (that's a neat trick; maybe there was an invisible pregnancy), uses the family invisibility drug to go unseen into Germany and fight a nasty Nazi, once again Sir Cedric Hardwicke (Sir Cedric must have been trying George Bernard Shaw's patience by now; Zeppo Marx was looking better and better, and Zeppo had retired from acting nine years before), and a fiendish Japanese baron, played by the great Hungarian actor Peter Lorre, who steals the whole film away from everyone, even the special effects, with his patented cold-blooded sadism, Mr. Moto as written by the Marquis DeSade. With the help of Ilona Massey, Griffin makes the world safe for freedom-loving invisible Americans everywhere. One wonders what H.G. Wells thought when he saw it, if he bothered to see any of these sequels to his novel. It is silly but it moves along fast, and it's entertaining. Peter Lorre is the only real reason to watch the film, but he's reason enough. Jon Hall lacks both charisma and a sufficiently distinctive voice.

Nevertheless, Hall was brought back for 1944's *The Invisible Man's Revenge*. Siodmak was gone, and someone at Universal remembered that the Invisible Man was supposed to be scary, not fighting Nazis, righting injustices, or giving Margaret Hamilton comic conniptions, and to do that, it helped if he was a bit on the insane side. Hall's Robert Griffin, a wholly different character from his Frank Griffin in *Invisible Agent*, isn't even related to the original Jack Griffin. His being named Griffin is just a *coincidence*. I'd call that an unbelievable coincidence if these weren't movies about people who are invisible.

Anyway, Robert Griffin is a revenge-crazed psychopath out seeking vengeance on a snooty family of British aristocrats he thinks have wronged him. Can you guess the primary target of his ire? Here are some hints. In *The Invisible Man Returns*, the invisible guy is out for revenge against Sir Cedric Hardwicke. In *Invisible Agent*, he's out to save the world from Sir Cedric Hardwicke. Sensing a trend? Yup, Hardwicke is being pursued by an invisible man implacably set on his destruction once again. How Hardwicke managed to avoid being the villain in *The Invisible Woman* escapes me. I imagine him sputtering to the producer: "What? I'm being chased around by a transparent guy yet *again*? I was in Hitchcock's *Suspicion*, H.G. Wells himself used me in his *Things to Come*! I'm *better* than this! Give this meshuggah role to Zeppo!"

Not having an invisibility serum as a family heirloom, Griffin luckily meets John Carradine, who had a minute role in *The Invisible Man* and who is now a mad veterinarian. Yes, that's right, a mad veterinarian, who apparently is making invisible pets for people with ugly doggies. Griffin is able to use his serum to become transparent, even though it's only been tested on animals. The effects are more sophisticated than before, and if the story isn't memorable, at least this invisible guy is enjoyably vicious once again. And John Carradine as a mad veterinarian? Come on. That's entertainment!

Universal's Invisible franchise ended up rather late, in 1952's *Abbott & Costello Meet the Invisible Man*, which just so happens to be the very first movie I ever saw. On the wall of the scientist's lab is a framed picture of Claude Rains, a respectful joke. (It would have been funnier to display a picture of an empty room, captioned "Granddaddy.") Abbott & Costello play inept private detectives who get involved helping an invisible boxer falsely accused of murder clear his name and unmask the real killer. (Let me be clear; they help an invisible boxer, not someone wearing invisible boxers, which would have made the movie unreleasable.)

 The Abbott & Costello film basically recycles the plot of *The Invisible Man Returns*. There's one classic sequence where Lou Costello is forced to box without knowing how with the Invisible Man landing all his punches for him, which works well until Lou accidentally knocks his invisible partner out cold. (When a young man, Lou Costello had actually been a boxer.) It ends with Lou helping his client become visible again with a transfusion and, ala *House of Dracula*, Lou gets some of the invisible blood, and half of his body turns invisible, which scares the comic hell out of him. I was not quite three years old when I saw it my first time in a movie theater, and that scene scared me as badly as Lou is scared onscreen. It was no gag to me at that age. I had nightmares about parts of my body disappearing.

 It's not a terribly funny movie, but it's a great deal better than *Abbott & Costello Meet the Mummy*, and for chubby chasers, Lou has his shirt off for the big boxing sequence.

THE BARELY VISIBLE MEN

The Invisible Man was the great Claude Rains' screen debut, but you only glimpse him in the final shot. Several other famous faces are barely glimpsed in this picture as well. Dwight Frye is wasted in a very small role as a reporter. John Carradine does a quick bit from behind a large mustache (his voice gives him away), formidable Violet Kemble Cooper shows up briefly, and Walter Brennan, shortly to win two Oscars, has a couple of lines in one scene.

17

NO MAN IS AN...
Island of Lost Souls (1932)

Are we not men?
— The Sayer of the Law (Bela Lugosi), genuinely curious

The Story

Shipwrecked Edward Parker (Richard Arlen) is picked up by a freighter transporting a load of caged animals (lions, tigers, Charles Gemora in a gorilla suit, jackals, dogs, etc.) to a remote island. The drunken, belligerent captain (Stanley Fields) abandons Parker on the island, which is a "biological research station" populated by the ugliest, most grotesque natives this side of the Molokai leper colony, and presided over by a mincing, utterly mad scientist named Dr. Moreau (Charles Laughton).

Responding to screams in the night, Parker sees what he thinks is Moreau and his "assistant" Montgomery (Arthur Hohl) vivisecting a living, conscious man. Parker flees into the woods and finds the native village, inhabited by grotesque, threatening monstrosities. Moreau arrives and shows that he rules these people, who are governed by a catechism of laws recited by a furry-faced beastman, the Sayer of the Law (Bela Lugosi).

Moreau shows Parker that the being he was vivisecting alive and conscious was not a man but an animal, like that makes it okay. He reveals that his experiments concern speeding up the process of evolution by surgically making ersatz humans out of animals. Perfectly reasonable mad science. What Moreau doesn't tell Parker is that the only woman on the island, Lota, is actually a panther, and Moreau wants to keep Parker around to see if Lota will respond to him sexually, since he and Montgomery are too gay for her. To this end, Moreau sinks his own boat.

In some place called Apia, Parker's fiancée Ruth has the British consul force the ship's captain to reveal where he marooned Parker. A rescue vessel is sent. The presence of Ruth on the island stirs up the natives, but it is Moreau ordering two natives to break his law not to spill blood, by killing the captain of the rescue ship, that riles them into a riot. The manimals decide that Moreau's order means the law is no more, so they kill Moreau by vivisecting him alive on his own operating table. Lota dies at the hands of one of the beast men, who succumbs to wounds suffered in the fight, allowing Parker, Ruth, and Montgomery to escape, while fire consumes the island of Dr. Moreau.

The Production

Erle C. Kenton, who later directed three of the Frankensteins, directed this rare example of Paramount poaching Universal's horror preserve, and cast the immensely talented gay British actor Charles Laughton as the very mad scientist. Lugosi was, as would be increasingly the case, cast in a small role to get his "marquee horror value" name in the credits.

Stanley Fields, who plays the gruff, mean captain who maroons Parker, had an interesting career. He was originally a comedian partnered with Frank Fay, the man who all but invented the traditional stand-up comedy monologist. (Fay was a hated man off stage, but brilliant onstage.) Among Fields' other film credits are Laurel & Hardy's sublime masterpiece *Way Out West*, the Laughton & Gable *Mutiny on the Bounty* (so this was not his last movie excursion to Catalina Island with Laughton), *Cimarron*, Wheeler & Woolsey's *Cracked Nuts* with Boris Karloff, *Little Caesar*, James Whale's *Showboat*, *Pack Up Your Troubles* with the Ritz Brothers, and two films that seem right at home here, *The Gay Desperado* and *The Devil Is a Sissy*. Fields was also the cousin of Spiro Agnew, but died long before Spiro disgraced his family and our nation.

Among the monsters hanging out with Lugosi, are Buster Crabbe (his great beauty cruelly disguised as ugliness) and Alan Ladd. The "gorilla" on the ship is gorilla-specialist actor Charles Gemora.

NO MAN IS AN...

The island coast scenes were shot on Santa Catalina Island. When I was a boy, shivering with fear as I first read the great Wells novel this movie is based on, Catalina was visible from our back yard. Had I known it was the Island of Dr. Moreau, how much more frightened would the book have made me?

The screenplay was by Waldemar Young and Phillip Wylie, just months, if not weeks, before Wylie's uncredited work on *The Invisible Man*.

What's Good About It

Island of Lost Souls has literate dialogue (thank you, Phil Wylie), ghastly torture, and just drips with unsavory, overwhelmingly unnatural sex. It's a potent mix, and the movie is still disturbing today, still scary.

Laughton's Moreau strides through his jungle, wielding a whip with expertise and arrogance. He is God here and he knows it and *loves* it! Laughton's performance is a treat. His Moreau is huge, expansive, bubbling with barely contained energy and high spirits. He is sly, mischievous, tyrannical, effeminate, perverted, and intelligent, sometimes all at once. Lugosi should have studied him, to see how to tap dance and cavort *on* the top without ever going all the way *over* the top. Laughton's performance is rich, and one can wallow in its playful fun amidst the horrors.

Bela is made-up a lot like the Wolfman will be some years later, with a face full of hair. Lugosi acts like crazy, throwing a million volts of energy back at Laughton as he brays Wells' abridged catechism through the hirsute face he wears. Looked at sanely, it is a terrible performance, but it works. He is supposed to be an animal mutilated into a wicked simulacrum of humanity, a parody of a man, so his performance's lack of any resemblance to a human being is right on the money. You can believe he is a thing that was never human, but that is trying to be human without knowing how. Lugosi's acting weaknesses here turn into strengths, and he's inadvertently effective.

The landing at Moreau's island has a great, spooky, foggy look. The film crew lucked out, because it was actually foggy when they shot the scenes over at Catalina, so it's all real fog.

Moreau's experiments are barbaric, pointless, and impossible. When Parker finds Moreau engaged in surgery on a conscious, screaming patient, it's as horrifying now as it was 80 years ago. In a panic, Parker runs out into the jungle night. It's damn scary in the book and it's damn scary in the movie.

When Lugosi gets his big speech, shrieked at the top of his lungs into Laughton's face, "You made us things! Not men! Not beasts! Part-man, part-beast. Thiiiiinnnngs!" it's Lugosi at his broadest and most over-the-top, his nose almost smudging the camera lens, but you can't laugh, because it's immediately followed by a succession of shots of monsters waggling up to close-ups, and they are all repulsive, scary, unsettling things.

What's Bad About It

It's occasionally ham-fisted. Ruth is kind of dull. Wells himself considered it a vulgarization of his novel. Maybe so. The book *is* better, but the film is still remarkably effective.

What's Gay About It

The handsome Richard Arlen's Parker, prime 1933 gay bait, is nursed back to dialogue by ex-doctor Montgomery. Montgomery takes one look at Arlen's seriously attractive carcass lying on the deck when they fish him out and instantly tells the shirtless crew members, "Take him to my cabin." Apparently Montgomery called shotgun. When asked if he's a doctor, Montgomery says, "Yes. At least I was, once upon a time." Clearly the man once made a *miscalculation*. Montgomery's use of the phrase "once upon a time" suggests we are in for a fairy tale. We are; a very dark one.

There is no romance in the book, except for Moreau and Montgomery, who are obviously a bitchy, gay married couple in both book and film. Laughton's Moreau is an effeminate queen, but he's clearly made the butcher Montgomery his bitch, and together they have an enormous brood of unnatural children. Paramount tried to heterosexualize the movie, but in so doing, they accidentally upped the gay ante tremendously.

In the book, there are just as many female manimals as male. In *The Island of Lost Souls*, there is Lota, "the only woman in the entire island." She's certainly Moreau's best work. She's an exotic beauty, clad in a bikini and doing kitty cat schtick that provides camp entertainment for Moreau, the voyeur, who lurks watching through the windows when he looses Lota to seduce Parker. Here we have literal voyeurism and bestiality running rampant on the screen. It's inconceivable that this would have passed the Motion Picture Production Code a few months later.

But by eliminating all the other female manimals from the story, they created a huge, exclusively male tribe of monsters. Surely we aren't supposed to believe that all of them, beasts with little concept of human homophobia, aren't humping each other right and left as they would be in nature. All higher mammals engage in homosexual activity in nature. Only man has invented the myth that it's unnatural. It is, in fact, very natural.

Moreau's response when Parker accuses him of barbarity is, "Mr. Parker, spare me these youthful horrors, please," flipping up his palm in a talk-to-the-hand gesture. He's an attitude queen sadist.

When Parker is about ready to make the man-beast-with-two-backs with Lota, he notices her claws are actually claws. He is furiously revolted, and rages up to Moreau, who is serving tea as effetely as he can, which is very, and Parker gives Moreau a good piece of his mind, absolutely *refusing* a cup of tea. When Moreau leers into a full facial close-up, mincing out his intentions to have Parker make some hot sexytime with Lota, Parker gay bashes him. My experience of straight guys is that if they find you have set them up with a hot babe, they're grateful. Parker's violent revulsion shows what team he really plays for, fiancée or not.

Inspecting Lota's claws, Moreau decides to drag her back to the House of Pain, vowing, "This time I'll burn out *all* the animal in her," and he laughs maniacally. He's Charles Laughton, so he makes it all work. Imagine Lugosi in the role.

After Moreau orders a murder, Lugosi confronts the moral conundrum and concludes, "Law no more," although this does do him out of a job. He becomes the Sayer of the No-Law.

The death of a "man like him" means to the monsters' amazement that "*he* can die!" All right! What are we waiting for? And for once, it's a mob of monsters who revolt, marching on the normals. In Moreau's gay ghetto, the straights are seriously outnumbered.

Moreau tries to re-establish his authority over his village people, but it's Stonewall night in the jungle. This is one of the great terrifying scenes of 1930s horror, one of the few that still raises hackles today, as this army of grotesque monsters pursues Moreau and slices him to ribbons with his own scalpels.

Aftermath

The film was too much for 1932, and did little business domestically. It was banned outright in England for decades, for being "against Nature." When told this, the beard of Dr. Moreau, Elsa Lanchester, replied, "So is Mickey Mouse."

It's been remade twice, once in a lackluster, forgettable version with Burt Lancaster (if you've made a forgettable version of *Island of Dr. Moreau*, you've really bungled it), and one with Marlon Brando, which is certainly not forgettable, much as its viewers might wish it was, being one of the most insane movies ever made, a truly hypnotically, jaw-droppingly terrible movie. It is awful in ways that can not be imagined. After over 80 years, *Island of Lost Souls* is still the best film version of Wells' terrifying novel.

18

BAD, SCIENCE, BAD!
Some Other Notable Mad Scientists

Dr. Mirakle
Bela Lugosi, *Murders in the Rue Morgue* (1932)

This is the movie Robert Florey made instead of *Frankenstein*. What a narrow escape *Frankenstein* had. It is a laughably bad movie. There's one clever touch; they use close-ups of a real ape, and keep the guy in the ape suit only for darkly lit long shots, resulting in the most believable ape character prior to *2001: A Space Odyssey*.

Sporting a Salma Hayek unibrow, Lugosi grossly overacts as a sideshow biologist whose big, ongoing experiment, in between his stage performances, is to kidnap women, inject them with ape's blood, waiting for one to survive, so he can mate his gorilla with her. Another perfectly reasonable experiment. Lugosi takes one look at simpering leading lady Sydney Fox and is filled with lust on his ape's behalf. He wants her for his monkey. Leon Ames saves the day with the help of his overweight, queeny "roommate." The imitation-German Expressionist sets look lovely.

Dr. Richard Vollin
Bela Lugosi, *The Raven* (1935)

My personal pick in the worst-ever Lugosi performance pool. This was the second Karloff-Lugosi co-starrer, and the only one where they made the error of giving the big, florid role to Lugosi and the smaller supporting role to Karloff.

Dr. Vollin is a mad plastic surgeon, obsessed with Edgar Allan Poe, whom he seems to feel needed vengeance against someone for something. Lugosi has tinkered together a collection of Poe torture devices, a mentally healthy hobby, and an early indication that he had his fingers crossed for the Hippocratic Oath.

From Lugosi's first appearance, unintelligibly garbling Poe's *The Raven*, Bela is off and running, building from wildly over-intense early madness to raving lunacy in just a few minutes. Some great acting performances are described as having "no false notes. Every moment rings true." Lugosi's Vollin has no true notes. Every moment rings ridiculous.

However, Lugosi receives competition from the extremely stupid screenplay. Dr. Vollin is madly ("madly" as in utterly deranged and insane) obsessed with a pretty young dancer named Jean Thatcher. Jean's father, Judge Thatcher (Samuel S. Hinds, who was also in *Son of Dracula*, and whose next movie after *The Raven* was my beloved nutso *SHE*), sees that Vollin is obsessed with his daughter, yet he begs him to operate on her when she's been injured. Yes, just who you want operating on your child, a madman obsessed with torture and her. When the Judge realizes that Vollin's feelings for Jean are not paternal, he delivers to Bela, with a straight face, one of the stupidest lines ever written. "You don't want a young girl like Jean falling in love with you." Judge Thatcher is so gay, he thinks all middle-aged men just *hate* having beautiful young women fall in love with them. Yeah. They hate that. Lugosi gives Thatcher the sensible-if-curt reply, "You driveling fool, stop talking!" Good idea.

But there's no sense at all in Lugosi's shrieking of his climactic aria, when Thatcher has a knife-pendulum swinging above him (*clearly* bolted to the ceiling crossbeams and unable to descend), and Jean and her boyfriend are trapped in a steel room where the walls are *slowly* coming together. (They come together with considerably more speed when Lugosi ends up in the room.) After contradicting himself in two sentences flat by saying, "I'm the sanest man who ever lived, but I will not be tortured. I tear torture out of myself by torturing *YOOOOOOOOUUUUUU!*" (very sane), he launches with all the force of his passionate Hungarian soul into, "What torture! What a delicious torture, Bateman, greater than Poe. Poe only conceived it. I have done it, Bateman! *POE, YOU ARE*

AVENGED!" followed by maniacal laughter like you've never seen unless you've seen this movie. I'd say he was acting his brains out, but I suspect he acted his brains out during a previous take, and that the shots in the finished film are the ones he did after his brains had gone walkabout. The movie has a moral, though; *never* employ a surgeon whom you know to be a raving sadist.

In 1962, Roger Corman made a film titled *The Raven*, also starring Boris Karloff, along with Peter Lorre, Vincent Price, and Jack Nicholson. It was an *intentional* comedy. It is very funny, but not as hilarious as 1935's *The Raven*, my choice for unintentionally funniest horror movie of the entire 1930s and '40s.

Dr. Gogol
Peter Lorre, *Mad Love* (1935)

Made and released at the same time as *The Raven*, MGM's *Mad Love* has much in common with it: a mad doctor obsessively in love with a woman who loves another, and a wild, broad performance in the role from a passionate Hungarian actor, often required to deliver silly speeches. Actor Ian Wolf is even in both movies. It's almost as camp and funny as *The Raven*, yet it is certainly a better movie. Why? Well, it was directed by *The Mummy*'s Karl Freund, photographed by *Citizen Kane*'s Gregg Toland, and the mad doctor is the great actor Peter Lorre in his American film debut. Plus, it has Colin Clive himself, as a mad pianist.

The exceptionally beautiful Francis Drake plays Yvonne Orlac, an actress who pretends to be tortured on stage every evening in Paris' *Le Théatre des Horreurs*. (Lugosi's Dr. Vollin would be disgusted by fake torture. "Where's her theatrical commitment?" he would ask.) The world's greatest surgeon (we're told this about him so definitively that one half-expects him to wear a ribbon sash with the title on it in glittery letters), Dr. Gogol, sits every evening, watching her faux torture through the narrowly parted curtains of his permanently reserved private box. When she shrieks in pretend agony, Lorre's briefly closed eyes tells us that he *enjoyed* her performance. One hopes he brought a towel.

You would think an intelligent, married actress would avoid a man who enjoys seeing her tortured every night, but when Yvonne's concert pianist husband, Stephen Orlac (Colin Clive), gets his hands crushed in a train wreck, she begs Dr. Gogol to repair them. I guess she thinks he watches her get tortured every single night for *wholesome* reasons. Gogol transplants the hands of a knife-throwing murderer (played by Edward Brophy, the voice of Timothy Mouse in Disney's *Dumbo*), whose execution by beheading Gogol had enjoyed earlier in the day. (Attending executions is Gogol's *other* hobby. They don't fake those.)

Gogol then launches a psychological campaign to convince the pianist Orlac that his hands want to *kill!* (Imagine if he'd given Orlac the hands of an habitual onanist. Those would be some memorable concerts!) In one bizarre scene, Gogol pretends to be the executed murderer Rollo, complete with mechanical hands, telling Orlac that Gogol *reattached his head*! Having played Henry Frankenstein (*Bride of Frankenstein* was shot that same year), naturally Colin Clive believed you can reattach a severed head and bring a dead man back to life. He does it himself all the time.

As if Gogol wasn't sufficiently peculiar already, he also buys a wax statue of Yvonne and talks to it (and does who knows what else with it). Needless to say, there's a scene at the climax where Yvonne pretends to be her own statue to hide from Gogol, after she's become painfully aware of his dishonorable intentions. Gogol is so nuts that when he notices his statue is bleeding, rather than realize that it's Yvonne, he thinks he's been granted his greatest wish, that his statue has come to life, like a hot Pinocchio. "You were wax but you came to life in my arms. ... My love has made you live! Galatea, give me your lips!" I hope he's asking for a kiss and not a lip transplant. The Lips of Orlac, they want to *KILL!*

Gogol confesses his big passion to Yvonne, raving, "I, a poor peasant, have conquered science. Why can't I conquer love? Don't you understand? You *must* be mine, not his. You *are* mine!" Oddly, this fails to win her heart.

So how does Peter Lorre play a crazy, over-the-top scientist and be great while Lugosi plays a similar role, just as big, and is laughable? There was Method in his madness. Lorre was a great actor, the favorite actor of the prominent German playwright Bertolt Brecht. Lorre plunged deep into his tortured characters' souls. He was what would later be called a method actor. When his characters raved and screamed, it welled up from deep inside him, bursting out no matter how hard he tried to hold it in. Lugosi made faces and belted his speeches, all technique, no depth. In Fritz Lang's brilliant movie *M*, Lorre raved and screamed and acted all over the place, in German, playing a revolting child-sex-murderer, and he rips your heart out. Lugosi could play a sympathetic tortured soul having the worst day of his life and be laughable, because it was all forced and artificial.

Additionally, there was the fact that Lorre knew what he was saying. Lugosi was acting in America for years without bothering to learn English, memorizing his lines phonetically. When Lorre interviewed with Alfred Hitchcock for his first English-language movie, the 1934 version of *The Man Who Knew Too Much*, the only English word he knew was "yes." So he listened to Hitchcock talk with a smile on his face, having no idea what Hitch was saying, and whenever a reply was expected, nodded and said, "Yes." He got the role, and then took intense private coaching in English. By the time *The Man Who Knew Too Much* went before the cameras, Lorre was fluent in English. Lugosi didn't bother. Knowing what you're saying can really help an acting performance.

Watch *The Raven* and *Mad Love* as a double feature, in either order. You'll laugh at both, but you won't laugh at Peter Lorre.

Dr. Janos Rukh

Boris Karloff, *The Invisible Ray* (1936)

In the movies, Francis Drake had unfortunate taste in men. Just four months after being Colin Clive's wife and Peter Lorre's wet dream, Francis found herself at Universal, playing the wife of Boris Karloff's mad Dr. Janos Rukh in the Karloff & Lugosi science-fiction thriller *The Invisible Ray*.

Universal had learned the lesson of *The Raven*. Karloff has the showy mad scientist role, which he could play without devouring the scenery, and Lugosi has the much smaller role of a sane, distinguished, nice scientist, which he played with admirable restraint. As a result, both Karloff and Lugosi are good in the picture.

Rukh is an intensely neurotic mad scientist who, like all mad scientists, lives in a huge castle high in the Carpathian mountains that looks like he bought it at Dracula's estate sale. He resides with his incredibly beautiful wife, Diane, and his annoyingly wise, strict, domineering mother (Violet Kemble Cooper). Years before, one of Janos' experiments blinded his mother, so Janos is carrying a load of Freudian guilt, making him a major mama's boy, the Clifton Webb of the Carpathians.

Diane Rukh, living on top of a mountain, ignored by her distracted husband, with nothing to do all day but be dominated by humorless Mother Rukh, is going batty with boredom. Naturally, when a party of scientists arrive, she picks out one of them and falls in love. That she picks Frank Lawton, fresh from playing the title role in MGM's *David Copperfield*, only shows how deeply desperate she was. The woman was *ravishing*. He's tepid Tapioca. She could do better.

Rukh becomes contaminated by radiation, so that he glows in the dark, very pretty, and his merest touch is deadly, not so pretty. Karloff is able to use the new element he's discovered to cure his mother's blindness, very Oedipally relieving.

Janos, whose always-shaky sanity is being further eroded by the radioactive poisons in his body, decides that *everyone* has betrayed him, and goes about touching folks.

Unfortunately, before he can rid his poor wife of her insipid, sexless lover, Mother Rukh practices a truly severe brand of tough love, by smashing the vials of chemicals he uses to keep the radiation from burning him up. Dominating to the end, she decides when he is to die, and humiliates him in front of a crowd of people in the process. Janos, like a good son, thanks his mommy for killing him, and jumps through a second-story window, bursting into a ball of flame as he does so. It's a spectacular exit from a special effects-heavy movie that is surprisingly less memorable than it sounds.

Dr. Ernest Sovac & Professor George Kingsley
Boris Karloff and Stanley Ridges, *Black Friday* (1940)

Kindly, loveable old absent-minded professor Kingsley gets hit by a car driven by a nasty gangster, Red Cannon, during a bungled getaway. At the hospital, brilliant brain surgeon Ernst Sovac, Professor Kingsley's best friend, aware than Cannon has half a million dollars in loot stashed away somewhere, performs a "brain transplantation" (the awkward term sounds like a southern ranch where slaves grow and pick brains, or like a farm which is changing genders) from Cannon into Kingsley. Now you'd think this would turn Kingsley into Cannon, and it does, but only part of the time. The rest of the time he's Kingsley's bumbly old self. (Where is his personality stored? In his liver?) Talk about absent-minded; his mind periodically goes so absent, another one fills in.

Throughout the rest of the movie Kingsley goes back and forth between his two personalities, nice Kingsley and rabid thug Cannon, with Sovac encouraging the personality reversion to try and find where Cannon has stashed the loot. (The Jekyll & Hyde aspect of this plot should move it into this book's third section, "The Beast Within," except it isn't Kingsley's inner nature surfacing; it's another person's evil self that's been surgically implanted in him, plus, hello, mad scientist, so it stays in this section.) Kindly Dr. Sovac is a tad reprehensible. If my best friend did this to me, I'd unfriend and block him.

Do you recognize the fine hand of Curt Siodmak at work here? Siodmak recycled much of this plot in his novel *Donovan's Brain*, only he replaced the silly brain "transplantation" with a far more believable disembodied-brain-kept-alive-in-a-tank-that-takes-possession-of-an-adjacent-scientist's-mind plot device. Isn't that better?

The original plan was for Karloff to play Kingsley and Lugosi to play Sovac. Good plan. Sovac, though obsessed, wildly irresponsible, and blatantly criminal (and also a lousy friend), is a restrained role. He has to appear sane at all times for his plan to work. Kinglsey is a real showboat role, a double personality, pure Jekyll & Hyde acting gold. Yet, for reasons I have not uncovered, Karloff decided to switch to the less showy role of Sovac. However, Lugosi was not switched into the Kinglsey role. He could not be trusted with showboat roles. His showboat was always the *Titanic*.

So a little-known actor named Stanley Ridges was cast as Kingsley, and did it quite well. Sadly for Bela, he was knocked back into playing Red Cannon's gangster rival, a *much* smaller role, and oddly, he had no scenes with Karloff. (Bela probably liked that.) He did get one over-the-top Bela scene, when he is trapped in a tiny closet and has a claustrophobic panic attack when left to suffocate. It's the usual Bela overplaying, but at least it's brief.

Dr. Henryk Savaard, Dr. Leon Kravaal, Dr. John Garth, Dr. Julian Blair

All Boris Karloff: *The Man They Could Not Hang* (1939), *The Man with Nine Lives* (1940), *Before I Hang* (1940), *The Devil Commands* (1941).

Columbia churned out this string of nearly identical pictures. The primary differences from film to film consist mainly of the various different wigs and facial hair Boris wears.

In *The Man They Could Not Hang*, Karloff's Dr. Savaard, when not shoveling more A's into his name, invents the perfect general anesthetic, death. (I imagine Drs. Vollin and Gogol saying "anesthetics are for pussies.") He wants to gas patients to death, operate on them, and then revive them. HMOs would love him, but I would want a second opinion. He kills a test subject but is arrested before he can revive him. Executed, he is resurrected by his loyal sidekick-lab assistant. Then he throws a dinner party for everyone he considers responsible, and begins murdering them, one by one, like Martha Stewart, only nicer.

In *The Man with Nine Lives*, Karloff's similarly overstocked-with-A's Dr. Kravaal is into cryonics. He wants to freeze people, operate on them, and then thaw them out. When he tries freezing someone, guess what happens. Yup. The cops show up, there's an accident, and they *all* get frozen. And that's all backstory, as the movie opens with the discovery of the cave full of frozen people ten years later. They thaw Karloff out, which turns out to be a bad idea, as he wants to use them for his next set of guinea pigs. Horror ensues.

In *Before I Hang*, Karloff's Dr. Garth is working on a rejuvenating serum. He commits a mercy killing and is sentenced to hang by the same judge who sentenced him to hang back in *The Man They Could Not Hang*. If that judge could only read his movie titles, he'd realize that Karloff would never be well hung. Karloff continues his experiments on his youth serum in prison, aided by Edward Van Sloan, who certainly could use it.

Karloff injects himself just before his scheduled hanging, not knowing his sentence has been commuted to life in prison, without the possibility of sequels. When he wakes up, he's twenty years younger. It would be a good, ironic joke on him, his having gratuitously given himself another twenty years in prison. Rod Serling would stop it right there if this were an episode of *The Twilight Zone*, but then Dr. Garth is pardoned, I assume for creating the greatest boon for aging narcissists ever. But, oops, he used the blood from a murderer (I mean from a *different* murderer, since Dr. Garth *is* a murderer; that's why he's in prison, remember?), and it turns into the "Blood of Orlac," as Garth's murderer blood starts him knocking off folks left and right. Darn that science.

In *The Devil Commands*, Karloff's Dr. Blair has discovered brain waves, and is recording different people's brain wave signatures. After his wife is killed in a traffic accident, his equipment begins recording her brain wave pattern from beyond the grave. Yeah, sure. Karloff becomes obsessed with trying to communicate with his wife in the next world, though he seldom listened to her when she was alive.

He takes live people and corpses he's stolen from a nearby cemetery (after all, Karloff studied Mad Science under Colin Clive, and Grave-Robbing 101 and 102 were required courses), puts them into weird metal hoods, and wires them together, along with a spirit medium, holding extremely bizarre scientific—and I use the word *very* loosely—séances to try to contact his dead wife. What could be more scientific? He seems finally to succeed, but it opens up a vortex—never a good sign—and he is sucked in and never seen again, much like any money spent to see these silly movies.

Dr. Marlow
Bela Lugosi, *Voodoo Man* (1944)

There are so many more mad scientists, I could do a whole book, and others have. I haven't touched on Lionel Atwill or George Zucco, though between the two of them, they played enough mad scientists to staff fully the faculty of Mad Cal Tech. I'm going to stop with *Voodoo Man*, which also has Zucco in it, and is about as basement-level as a mad scientist movie can get. This movie aspires to be a B-movie, but it will need to work a lot harder even to make it to a C-movie.

Lugosi's wife is a zombie, to no one's surprise, and Lugosi and his cohorts, Zucco and John Carradine, kidnap women, like you do, to use in mad experiments involving voodoo and science, a natural pairing, like chocolate and uranium, to try to revive the zombie wife. Try getting a research grant for this project. Lugosi is relatively dignified in this, as opposed to Zucco in voodoo priest robes complete with feathers and face paint, chanting "Rambana never fails," and other equally meaningful verbiage. I might add, though, that Rambana never succeeds in this movie, either. And poor John Carradine. This man, who played the great roles of Shakespeare on stage, here plays a low-functioning moron, with oily hair hanging in his face as he listlessly plays a bongo drum during the experiments/ceremonies, like Maynard G. Krebs from *Dobie Gillis* after a lobotomy. This film is terrible.

So remember, science is bad, and Rambana never fails.

THE MAD SCIENCE QUIZ

(33% of your grade. Answers at the back of the book.)

1. What was Mary Shelley's full name?
2. Mary's mother was also a famous writer. What was the name of her most famous work and what was its subject?
3. *Frankenstein* was remade in 1957 by Hammer Studios, and again in 1994, produced by Francis Ford Coppola. What were the titles of these movies, who played the monster and who played Dr. Frankenstein in each?
4. Why does the Frankenstein Monster have a flat head?
5. Basil Rathbone, Boris Karloff, Peter Lorre, and Vincent Price eventually all appeared together in one movie. What was the title of that movie, who directed it, who wrote it, who produced it, and when did it come out?

PART THREE
The Beast Within

What do you think of at night when you go to bed, you beast
— Captain Jeffrey T. Spaulding (Groucho Marx)
getting nosy in *Animal Crackers*

Sex feels good (If you're doing it right), but then so does a hot bath or a massage. Yet few people propose a lifetime's commitment to their masseur or masseuse. The real intimacy of sex isn't sharing our anatomy; it's revealing our hidden, inner selves.

An openly gay high school student was unthinkable in the 1960s. There were no gays on TV; Paul Lynde was just funny, and he kept on playing suburban fathers. Clifton Webb, who was clearly gay, not only kept playing dads, but in *Cheaper by the Dozen*, we were supposed to believe he had fathered *twelve* children by Myrna Loy. Clifton Webb and Paul Lynde had secret second lives. So did Henry Jekyll and Larry Talbot. They are the lynch pins of a whole genre of monster movies about our beasts within.

Dr Henry Jekyll is a proper, repressed Victorian gentleman who takes a drug which eradicates his inhibitions and unleashes his id, turning him into a libidinous monster who hightails it to London's seediest dens of iniquity where he indulges in vice, crime, sadism, violence, and ultimately murder. And he does it for *fun*!

Lawrence Talbot, the Wolfman, was another matter. One night a girl is attacked by what all concerned believe is a wolf, but which is actually a werewolf. Talbot tries to save the girl and is bitten. He now finds himself turning into a wild beast of an evening, and goes on the prowl for victims on whom to unleash his bloodlust. He hates himself in the morning, and wants only to die.

Ever felt like Larry Talbot on a full moon? Ever popped, drunk, snorted, smoked, or injected anything that unleashed *your* Edward Hyde? I thought so. You have a beast within. You're a monster.

19

THE DOCTOR WILL KILL YOU NOW

Doctors Jekyll & Misters Hyde

The only way to get rid of a temptation is to yield to it.
— Oscar Wilde, being truthful in *The Picture of Doran Gray*

Frankenstein, or the Modern Prometheus began as a nightmare Mary Shelley had in 1816, which led her to invent the whole mad scientist genre. Eighty or so years later, another nightmare inspired Bram Stoker to write his 1897 novel *Dracula*.

It was also a nightmare that spurred Robert Louis Stevenson to knock out *The Strange Case of Dr. Jekyll and Mr. Hyde* (1886) in just *three days*! Then he was so horrified by it, he burned it, but the story so possessed him that he took another three days and wrote it again. Wise decision. *Jekyll & Hyde* is still remembered and read today as much as his *Treasure Island*.

Jekyll certainly qualifies as a mad scientist, but I placed him in this section of the book because he is very much a man who unleashed his beast within.

The tale has been filmed so many times, it's not possible to compile a definitive list of every movie made from or inspired by it. One of my favorite variations was Hammer's 1972 transgender classic, *Dr. Jekyll and Sister Hyde*, in which Ralph Bates' Jekyll takes a potion that turns him into Martine Beswicke's voluptuous Sister Hyde. (Talk about your gay "overtones"!)

In 1986, Miss Beswicke revisited her Sister Hyde character in a one-time-only stage comedy sketch in Hollywood titled *Dr. Jekyll's Brother Meets Sister Hyde's Sister*. Martine again played Sister Hyde and her new Doctor Jekyll was the humble author of this trifling work. Let me tell you, a potion that would turn men into Martine Beswicke would *sell*! I know. I did it!

Paramount shot a very good version in 1931 for which Fredric March won the Oscar for Best Actor, an award not won by a horror performance again for sixty years. In 1941, MGM shot almost the same script with Spencer Tracy, a great but quintessentially American actor, as the posh English Dr. Jekyll; Lana Turner, a quintessentially American talent-free mannequin, as an upper-class English woman; and Ingrid Bergman, a voluptuous and enormously talented Swede, as a cockney slattern.

The directing chores were handled by Victor Fleming, a virile, machismo-drenched, straight, recreational hunter best remembered for directing the gayest movie of all, *The Wizard of Oz*.

Spencer Tracy, in his wisdom, doesn't even attempt an accent. He plays one of the many posh Mayfair doctors who happen to have a Wisconsin accent. Lana Turner follows Tracey's lead, and then takes it one step further, attempting neither an accent nor a performance. As usual, her primary concern is displaying her wardrobe to maximum effect. Ingrid Bergman has an accent all right, so strong she's barely intelligible, but it does not suggest she was born within the sound of Bow Bells. What it suggests is that she spent her formative years seeing the sun only six months out of every twelve.

Fleming's *Jekyll & Hyde* just sits there on the screen, presenting its weird, American England, with a Mr. Hyde who is just Dr. Jekyll grimacing while wearing a fright wig. It's not particularly scary nor atmospheric. It isn't much of anything except an example of MGM's hubris.

Dr. Jekyll is good; Mr. Hyde is evil. That's the most basic accepted fact about this story. But is it a fact? I'll grant that Hyde is evil, but just how "good" is Dr. Henry Jekyll, no matter who is playing him?

The first time he takes the drug, it's an "experiment." Sure. All reputable scientists experiment on themselves. But from the second dose on, he is taking the drug voluntarily, for recreation. Jekyll becomes Hyde's hideout, his disguise. In the climactic scene, Jekyll clings to his good guy identity, which is decaying as he speaks, to avoid the consequences of Hyde's crimes.

Are those the actions of a good man?

Jekyll takes the drug because it's *fun*. It obliterates his inhibitions. He has a good time as Hyde. Hyde parties hardy. Jekyll knows what he's doing. He has no memory loss. He's well aware that he's out torturing little cockney guttersnipe Ingrid Bergman every night, cheating on good girl/clothes-horse Lana, but he keeps doing it because he enjoys it.

Is this your idea of a good guy?

When Ingrid confronts Jekyll with her misery, the sub-atomic particle of a conscience he has left feels a quark-sized pang, and he promises Hyde will never bother her again. She goes home relived, where Hyde kills her.

Does Jekyll turn himself in? Nope. When the police come looking for Hyde, Jekyll tries desperately to pretend someone else committed those crimes.

Dr. Jekyll is a schmuck, who, after performing an experiment as morally repugnant as it is ethically and scientifically dubious, invents an imaginary justification for his revolting pastimes, and then indulges all his worst impulses. When he tries to rehabilitate himself, he finds he is addicted, that the transformations come on their own, and he needs the drug to regain himself. His story is that of a man who destroys himself, along with a cluster of contiguous innocents, for pleasure.

Hank Jekyll's tale can be seen as a tale of drug addiction. He takes a drug for the pleasure of removing his inhibitions and losing all civilized restraint, becomes a licentious beast, becomes a hypocrite, pretending to a morality he slips on and off like a robe, finds he is desperately addicted, commits crimes, first for fun, then to escape justice, and when the drug is used up, he dies.

What about you? Have you ever unleashed your Mr. Hyde? Have you ever taken refuge behind your Dr. Jekyll façade?

Are you ever a monster, just for the night?

20

WHERE WOLF?
Werewolf of London (1935)

> *This mediaeval unpleasantness.*
> — Wilfred Glendon (Henry Hull),
> being dismissive of his own curse

The Story

Irritable English botanist Wilfred Glendon, while in Tibet seeking a rare flower that only blooms under the full moon, is bitten by a werewolf. Once back in England, he is stalked by a mysterious Asian doctor named Yogami, who tells him that this flower is the only antidote for the curse of the werewolf.

Glendon's bored wife Lisa begins seeing an old suitor, which inflames Glendon's jealousy. When the full moon rises, Glendon turns into a manbeast and stalks the London fog, killing all he encounters.

When he tries to use his flower to stem the curse, he finds that Dr. Yogami has stolen the blooms. Glendon confronts Yogami, who is the werewolf who bit him in Tibet, and kills him. Then he attacks his wife and her lover, but is shot by the police.

The Production

Universal's first shot at a werewolf movie was this notorious near-miss. Despite the movie's title, you'll search in vain for any glimpse of familiar London landmarks. Like *Dracula*, it's all shot on the Universal lot. *Dracula* at least had one stock shot of Trafalgar Square. They do have British actors playing the denizens of London, unlike MGM's Midwestern version of London in *Dr. Jekyll and Mr. Hyde*. This movie only ventures off the lot when they employ the Vasquez Rocks north of Los Angeles for Tibet.

Dr. Glendon may not be a mad scientist (though a Mad Botanist sounds like fun), but he's a pretty angry scientist through most of the picture.

Watching it, one can't help thinking how much better it would be if Boris Karloff had played Wilfred Glendon and Bela Lugosi had played Dr. Yogami. Lugosi was not Japanese, but Warner Oland, who played the role, and who had played two prominent Asian roles, Fu Manchu and Charlie Chan, was Swedish.

But Karloff wasn't available, as *Bride of Frankenstein* was still in production when cameras turned on this picture. Valerie Hobson, who was the heroine in both, on some days had to shoot scenes for each of them. Without Karloff's name to link with Lugosi's, Universal saw no reason to give this plum role to Lugosi, though it's likely he could have been good in the part.

What's Good About It

Although Warner Oland is miscast, he is still kind of fun. And Glendon makes a natty werewolf. *After* transforming into the beast, he puts on a coat, cap, and scarf. This werewolf won't go a-prowling until he is properly attired and accessorized.

There's lots of comic relief to be had. Gay actress Spring Byington has several comic scenes as a daffy society hostess. Ethel Griffies, the tweedy dykish ornithologist in Hitchcock's *The Birds* nearly thirty years later (she seems to be the same age in both movies; she was one of those people who are born old), and Zeffie Tilbury play relentless comedy scenes as a couple of drunken, cockney, lesbian hags, Mrs.Whack and Mrs. Moncaster. No, Mrs. Whack isn't offed.

Glendon actually gets to say, "Lock me in. Don't open that door before sunrise. Even if I call, pay no attention to it. Keep that door locked till dawn."

What's Bad About It

Henry Hull was not a charismatic actor. He's tiresome, stagy, and annoying. This holds true for his performances in *Great*

Expectations (grossly miscast as the convict Magwitch), Hitchcock's *Lifeboat*, and even Vincent Price's *Master of the World*. And on top of that, he considered himself above such trash, yet he fails to rise up to it. A better director would have helped immensely as well.

You know, there's only one full moon a month on this planet, but the moon must have paused in its orbit in 1935, because in *Werewolf of London*, the moon is full on three consecutive nights.

The movie is poorly paced, and fails to find the pathos that would later make Larry Talbot so memorable. Hull truly can not evoke pathos.

What's Gay About It

This movie about a fierce rivalry between two werewolves who bring out the worst in each other was written by gay screenwriter John Colton. The skimpy plot is built around the sexual dynamic of Glendon, Yogami, Lisa, and Lisa's old boyfriend, Paul. Glendon becomes increasingly jealous of his wife's relationship with Paul throughout the film, while Yogami relentlessly stalks Glendon. Glendon tries to charm his wife's affection back by issuing unilateral orders to her, which she ignores.

Yogami tells Glendon that he and Glendon met "in Tibet once, but only for a moment, in the dark," as he caresses Glendon's wolf-bitten arm. In other words, during anonymous public sex, when Yogami was the rough beast who left Glendon scarred and cursed. When the wife enters, Yogami takes his hand off Glendon and plays straight for her, but there's nothing in the film to indicate that Yogami likes girls.

During one attack, Paul recognizes Glendon in his werewolf form. How embarrassing, like running into a friend from work at a porn theater. He's easily recognized because he wears minimal monster make-up, Hull having refused to wear the full Larry Talbot face Jack Pierce had intended to give him.

At the climax, Glendon blames Yogami for turning him gay. "You brought this on me that night in Tibet." Now, now; no finger-pointing. Take some personal responsibility, Wilfred. Glendon's beast side comes out and he tries to rape Yogami. Yes, they've flip-flopped, a sure sign of true love, but Glendon plays too rough, doesn't understand Yogami's Japanese safe word, and Yogami dies.

Glendon then assaults his wife's lover. There are actually a couple of shots of Paul lying face down with Glendon, in his wolf drag, on top of him, grunting and growling with pleasure. The wife catches her men betraying her with each other and has a hissy fit, like she hasn't been dancing on the edge of infidelity for the entire movie herself. Glendon tries to silence her by eating her, but is interrupted by the police, who kill him with a regular bullet. No silver bullet required in this werewolf tale.

Aftermath

This disappointing film sparked no sequels, and certainly failed to make a horror icon of dreary Henry Hull. It would be another six years until Lon Chaney Jr. made a werewolf the popular equal of Frankenstein and Dracula.

21

A DOG'S LIFE
The Wolf Man (1941)

Even a man who is pure in heart...
— The entire cast of *The Wolf Man*, one by one, reciting the only poem anyone there knows

The Story

After the death of his older son, Sir John Talbot of Lanwelly, Wales, summons his estranged younger son, Lawrence, home to prepare to assume the duties of the heir apparent to the Talbot estates and title. While on a date with a village girl, Gwen Conliffe, to visit a gypsy encampment, Larry tries to save a young woman being attacked by what looks like a wolf (well, what looks like a German shepherd), and is bitten by the animal, which he beats to death with a silver-headed cane.

The wolf was Bela the Gypsy in werewolf form, and the bite passes the curse to Larry, who finds himself turning into a half-man/half-wolf every evening and killing folks. Why Bela becomes a full German shepherd, excuse me, wolf, while Larry becomes a humanoid man-wolf is never addressed.

Larry is unable to convince anyone he is guilty of the string of murders. His father becomes convinced that Larry is insane. When Gwen is attacked by the beast, Sir John beats the creature to death with Larry's silver-headed cane, only to see the animal transform back into his son at his feet.

The Production

Curt Siodmak was a Jew born in Dresden, Germany. Having fled the Nazis under harrowing circumstances that turn his autobiography into a gripping read, he knew what monstrous beasts lurked within the breasts of average people. In his memoir, he refers to the Nazis as "Wolf People," and when he was assigned to write *The Wolf Man*, he wrote a story informed by his experience of folks who were really wolves deep inside. It is not a coincidence that the picture is full of people who are marked for death with a star, only with five points instead of six. Siodmak's timing couldn't have been more on the nose. *The Wolf Man* was released just five days after the bombing of Pearl Harbor. The full moon had risen and the Wolf People were on a rampage.

The Universal backlot sets used for the village of Lanwelly still stand today. Known as "The Court of Miracles," it is often included on the Universal tour. A few years ago, I was privileged to tool about the Universal lot on a golf cart, and to get off and romp on the sets. Although standing on Norman Bates' front porch and knocking on the door of the Bates House was the day's biggest thrill, a close second was walking about the Court of Miracles, and being photographed standing where so often I've seen Larry Talbot prowl.

What's Good About It

The Wolf Man is a B-movie that looks like an A-picture, thanks primarily to a first-rate cast, including Bela Lugosi, Ralph Bellamy, Maria Ouspenskaya, beautiful Evelyn Ankers, Warren William, dreamy Patric Knowles, and the wonderful Claude Rains, fully visible now. Lon Chaney Jr. has his best role, and is excellent in the part. The wolf is played by a German shepherd named Moose. Chaney took a shine to Moose and bought him. He appears in a number of Chaney's movies, and went to the studio with his master every day for the rest of the dog's life.

It is one of Siodmak's best scripts, though there's nary a brain transplant in sight. Siodmak is even the author of the convincingly authentic-sounding doggerel recited by nearly every character in the movie.

> Even a man who is pure in heart,
> And says his prayers by night,
> May become a wolf when the wolfbane blooms,
> And the autumn moon is bright.

You may notice there is no mention of the full moon. The idea that he turns into a wolf on full moons was not introduced until *Frankenstein Meets the Wolfman*. There is no moon in this movie. Larry can transform pretty much any and every night, so long as it's autumn.

Larry Talbot is the son of a Welsh nobleman, but Siodmak, never a fan of Chaney's acting anyway (as he makes clear in his book), carefully established that Larry had been living in California for eighteen years, to account for his American accent. Lon makes a convincing Californian. And as long as I'm on the topic of accents, though Rains, Knowles, Warren William, and dependable Doris Lloyd all have lovely, real English accents, and Maria Ouspenskaya's gypsy accent convinces (though it's really a Russian accent), no one in the entire picture even attempts a Welsh accent. Ankers and Bellamy, of course, sound like they have been living in California with Larry Talbot.

Little is required of Bela Lugosi in *The Wolf Man*. He plays a character from his own homeland, so his accent is authentic. He wears little character make-up beyond a wig and a pasted-on mustache. He isn't even required to learn a new first name. He's in the film for five minutes, and he only speaks seven lines. He's good. (A stunt double plays him when his character drives a gypsy horse caravan through the Court of Miracles.)

Larry starts out the film charmingly loutish, but as the picture progresses, he grows aware of his curse, begs others for help, only to be told repeatedly that he is imagining it, and his desperation and misery, compounded by guilt over the mounting pile of people he's killed, grows enormous. Chaney brings it all off convincingly and touchingly, as well as being vicious and bestial in his scenes in the monster make-up.

And while we see him transform while wearing a tank-top undershirt, only to cut to shots of the Wolfman prowling in a brown, long-sleeved, fully buttoned shirt, at least, unlike with Wilfred Glendon, we don't actually *see* the beast choosing which shirt to wear, then putting it on, and buttoning it all the way up to the collar, the way animals always do. (The reason for the long sleeves and the full buttoning up is, of course, so that they didn't have to cover his chest and arms with more yak hair.)

What's Bad About It
The movie stardom of Warren William seems inexplicable to me. His Julius Caesar in DeMille's *Cleopatra*, his turn as a leading man for Mae West in *Go West, Young Man*, and his string of films as Perry Mason, are all bewilderingly dull performances to my eyes and ears. His uninteresting work in *The Wolf Man* is of a piece with those others. Ralph Bellamy, who developed into a fine actor, shows little promise of it here, though he is energetic. His Captain Montford is a surprisingly coarse and crass man for what is supposed to be a sympathetic character. The movie's pacing falters a bit in the middle.

And then there's the overwhelmingly wizened old gypsy crone Maleva, played by Maria Ouspenskaya. Maria's reputation as a great actress takes a beating from this tremendously camp performance. My theater professor back in college would giggle with glee whenever she was mentioned, and launch into his hilarious impersonation of her. Also, Maria is supposed to be Bela's mother, but Maria was actually five years younger than Lugosi, though she certainly doesn't look it.

What's Gay About It
Once cursed, Larry goes out prowling the night, cruising for people on whom to satiate his unspeakable lusts. The next morning, Larry is appalled by what he has done. He seeks advice from his father about it.

But Rains is no help. He is convinced his son is mentally ill. Well, it was 1941; the American Psychiatric Association still classified lycanthropy as a mental disease back then. Warren William's Dr. Lloyd also assures Larry that werewolves are merely mentally sick perverts. Bellamy's Captain Montford takes a predictable hard-line approach. He only wants to shoot the beast. "Just imagine having a stuffed werewolf staring at you from the wall," he says. Montford is organizing hunters, and probably sending undercover officers into public men's rooms, to flush out this threat to the family. Larry does set off the villagers' gaydar, and whenever Larry goes out in public, there's a good deal of finger-pointing, glaring stares, and disapproving whispers. Also, dogs bark at him and cats hiss.

Animals can be so homophobic. When he visits Maleva in the gypsy camp for help, the gypsies, who *know* what he is, pack up and get out of town in record time.

And every time Larry tries coming out of the closet to anyone, they refuse to believe him. He doesn't conform to their stereotype of a gay werewolf. He's very butch. In essence, the conversation constantly repeated is, "Dad, I'm gay."

"No, you're not. No son of mine could be gay. You're just sensitive. Butch up. Shake it off." Ladies and gentleman, my dad.

Sir John even tries homemade bondage to cure his son, tying him to a chair for a night, while he goes off to hunt for the real pervert. When Larry finally makes the attack on Gwen that we all knew was coming from the opening credits, it is Sir John who comes to the rescue, beating the furry homo to death with the phallic wolf's head cane, only to be appalled afterwards, when he sees it's his own son he's gay-bashed. Oops.

Aftermath

The Wolf Man is a good-looking film, with a particularly atmospheric foggy forest set (on a sound stage). Siodmak's psychological approach makes it a Greek tragedy (he states flat-out in his autobiography that he was writing a Greek tragedy) in monster movie guise that everyone can relate to. Gay or straight, we all have beasts within. The movie was a big hit, and Larry Talbot went on to appear in four more movies. But before we look at those, we'll take a quick look at RKO's feminine feline response.

22

PUSSY GALORE
Cat People (1942)

I never cease to marvel at what lies behind a brownstone front.
— Oliver Reed (Kent Smith), speaking in metaphors

The Story

Fashion designer Irena Dubrovna marries ship designer Oliver Reed. On their wedding night, Irena keeps Oliver locked out of her bedroom. She's terrified of having sex with him, because she believes that if she does, she will turn into a panther and eat him. When Oliver learns his wife won't have sex with him, he decides she's crazy and sends her to a psychiatrist, who also thinks she's insane, because she won't have sex with *him*, either.

Meanwhile, Oliver blabs all of his and Irena's most intimate sexual problems to his friend Alice at work. Irena grows jealous, and Alice finds herself being stalked through Central Park and in an outdoor swimming pool by some creature in the shadows that growls and screeches like a panther.

Her psychiatrist sexually assaults Irena, only to have her turn into a snarling panther in his arms. He manages to stab her with a sword before dying. She frees a real panther from the zoo next door, which kills her, while allowing the police to think the escaped beast killed the unethical shrink. Oliver is so grief stricken, he marries Alice.

The Production

Curt Siodmak wasn't specifically writing about sex when he created Larry Talbot; he was writing about Nazis, but when Val Lewton made *Cat People* over at RKO a year later, he *was* making a movie about sex, about the way that sex can awaken the beast within you, and about being terrified of awakening your beast.

Val Lewton ran the RKO B-movie unit in the 1940s. They had quite a unique system. The front office, the scared survivors of the executive purge following the failure of *Citizen Kane* (in what was a clear slap in the face of Orson Welles, they'd adopted the slogan "Showmanship not Genius"), would invent what they felt was a marketable title, usually as lurid as they could come up with, and hand it to Lewton, saying, "Make a movie with this title, and here's your tiny budget." Lewton would then make a brilliant, shadowy, intellectual thriller that was over the heads of the studio brass whose very slogan displayed contempt for genius.

RKO saw *The Wolf Man* rake in cash for Universal, so they covetously imagined a cat woman, and handed Lewton the title *Cat People*, expecting shortly to see a furry-faced starlet stalking himbos through the fog. When they saw the finished film, they were flummoxed. There wasn't even a monster. Lewton, writer DeWitt Bodeen, and director Jacques Tourneur had left it ambiguous as to whether or not Irena, the pussy person played with exquisite charm by the redundantly named French actress Simone Simon, actually turned into a panther or not. The studio insisted on inserting a panther into a few shots, but Lewton kept it in shadows and preserved his ambiguity.

B-movies were often the beneficiaries of A-movies' leftovers. In the case of *Cat People*, the magnificent huge stairway in Irena's building is from the Amberson mansion of Orson Welles' recently aborted, yet still brilliant, production of *The Magnificent Ambersons*, left behind in the studio's abrupt divorce from Mr. Welles.

What's Good About It

It's intelligent, subtle, psychologically interesting, scary, and downright weird in parts. It looks great. Simone Simon is charming.

Tom Conway is a wonderfully smarmy smoothie as the unethical psychiatrist, Dr. Judd, and Lewton regular Elizabeth

Russell contributes a terrifically off-kilter, memorably creepy bit as another cat woman who recognizes Irena as her "sister."

In the justly famous sequences where Alice finds herself being stalked through the park and in a dark hotel swimming pool by something that meows menacingly, shadows and sound effects create terror out of nothing. The sure hand of director Jacques Tourneur is at work there.

What's Bad About It

This "Oliver Reed" isn't the sexy drunken movie star of the same name, but rather is the stunningly sexless and boring Kent Smith, a man somewhat less erotically exciting than overcooked tapioca pudding, and a less-than-riveting actor. Irena is convinced that if she gets sexually aroused, she'll turn into a panther and eat him, turning Oliver into food, glorious food. That she might be better off if she does never occurs to her.

Jane Randolph as Alice isn't actually bad, but next to the delightful sex kitten Simone Simon, she might as well be a tree or a scratching post.

What's Gay About It

It's a movie about being afraid of sex, and it turns out the sexophobe is right. Show me a gay person who doesn't know how dangerous, how deadly, their sex drive is. It presents heterosexuality as a pretty bad idea. And it's full of pussy imagery.

Dr. Judd is a grossly unethical quack. Not only does he tell his patients' secrets to everyone he meets, but when Irena tells him she doesn't want to kiss him, he threatens to have her committed. He's about as charming a ladies man as Bill Cosby. He's yet another male who thinks a woman who doesn't desire him is insane.

Oliver whines about how Irena's terror of sex is especially awful for *him* because he's never had anything go wrong in his life before, and doesn't know how to cope with not always getting everything he wants. By this point, most of the audience would like to see him clawed to death also. That Irena dies is tragic. That this spoiled, whiny boob survives, remarries, and lives happily ever after, doubles the tragedy.

Oliver is surprised that Irena gets upset when he mentions how he'd told Alice all their intimate secrets. "Oh, you can tell Alice anything. She's such a good egg she can understand anything," the insensitive, thick-headed moron jabbers. Then he takes Alice along on a museum outing with Irena, and suggests Irena go off upstairs and leave he and Alice alone. Oliver is an idiot.

Inevitably, Judd tells Irena that her fears that sexual arousal will turn her into a panther are just delusions, and to prove it, he kisses her, and she eats him. This is usually seen as proving him wrong in a blackly comic touch, but I must disagree. Getting kissed by smug, smarmy Dr. Judd is about as sexually arousing as frostbite. Between slimy Dr. Judd and thick-headed sexless Oliver, it seems to me that it is sexual *revulsion* that turns Irena into a beast, and so one cheers her on.

Watching this movie again to write this chapter, I found myself wondering, does Irena really fear that sex with Oliver will awaken her beast within or, far, far worse, does she fear it *won't*?

Aftermath

The studio released *Cat People* with trepidation, but it was a huge hit, and Lewton made eight more brilliant, moody shockers, including *Curse of the Cat People*, which had no cat people at all.

23

FAMILY DIES: THE CHANEYS
Lon Chaney (1883–1930)
Creighton (Lon Jr) Chaney (1906–1973)

Feast your eyes; glut your soul on my accursed ugliness!
— Erik (Lon Chaney), taking an unusual approach to wooing a woman, in *The Phantom of the Opera*.

But that's the secret of life. What good does it do me? I'm not interested in life. I wasn't created artificially, I'm a human being. I've got real blood in my veins. What can we do to end my life?
— Larry Talbot (Lon Chaney Jr), who thinks it's all about him, in *Frankenstein Meets the Wolfman*.

In the 1920s, Lon Chaney was one of the greatest of all movie stars. But sound came in and Lon died, almost simultaneously, and Lon's films were put aside, and except for *The Phantom of the Opera* and *The Hunchback of Notre Dame*, he was forgotten by several generations. Ironically, his less-talented son who usurped his name was better remembered.

Nowadays, thanks to DVD, most of Lon's surviving movies are readily available, and they are a revelation. Lon Chaney was a *great* actor. It's hard for young people today, watching the broad, melodramatic, gesticulatory style of acting in silent films, to see past the almost camp overacting, but not with Chaney.

Watch *The Unknown*, with Chaney and Joan Crawford. His performance as Alonzo (Lon's real name), the armless knife-thrower (yes, you read that right), will amaze you, horrify you, rip at your heart, and move you. He's *incredible*!

Watch *The Penalty*, where he plays the legless crime boss Blizzard. Blizzard's plot to conquer San Francisco with an army of anarchists is absurd (for one thing, it's tremendously hard to instill command discipline in anarchists), but Chaney's ruthless, brutal gangster out-Bogarts Humphrey Bogart. This guy would scare James Cagney. Even without Chaney's masochistic playing of the entire role on his knees, with his feet strapped to his butt (I'm not joking), it would still be amazing.

There is a recurrent theme in all of Chaney's movies: unrequited love. In almost every movie he is in love with some woman who will never love him back because, even without the grotesque make-ups that were his trademark, he was no Hugh Jackman. Often this twists him into a vicious monster who plots horrible fates for his romantic rivals, but just as often, he is redeemed by his love to acts of noble self-sacrifice. Sometimes both. In *The Unknown*, he tries to have romantic rival Norman Kerry's arms torn off by horses, only to throw himself under the horse's hooves to save Joan Crawford. Bette Davis might have advised him not to bother.

Time and again, through hideous make-ups, distorted bodies, and a long outdated acting style, he reaches out and touches your heart. He's magnificent.

Most of the people who knew Lon Chaney spoke admiringly of him. My grandfather worked with him on several films, and spoke glowingly to me of a fine, kind man. Conversely, Curt Siodmak accused him of sadistic cruelty in the way he raised his son. However, Siodmak never met Lon. My grandfather was his friend. I'll take my granddad's informed word on the matter.

Certainly Lon could be distant. He didn't make the Hollywood social rounds, and was happiest in a cabin he built in the mountains, far from people or roads. His first wife, Cleva, Creighton's mother, was sufficiently unhappy with him that she went to a theater where he was performing one night, and drank bichloride of mercury in the stage wings. After the divorce, Lon never saw nor spoke to or of her again.

Lon Chaney was 47, and signed to play Count Dracula, when he died of throat cancer on August 26, 1930.

Creighton Chaney liked to tell the story of his being born in Oklahoma City in February, 1906, dead, and of his father rushing outside with his baby son in his arms, to plunge the infant into an icy river, shocking him into life. It's a great story. But Creighton also liked to tell people he had played both roles in *Frankenstein Meets the Wolfman*. Creighton liked a good story, and he never let truth get in the way of one. Maybe it happened.

Lon did *not* want his son to be an actor. That Creighton would eventually find fame as "Lon Chaney Jr" would have appalled Lon.

Creighton was never the great actor his father was, and that shadow was a heavy burden. But neither was he the lousy actor his worst work suggests. His performance as Lenny in *Of Mice and Men* was brilliant. Watching it, one is hard-pressed to believe this is the actor with that same face and voice who was in *The Alligator People* or *The Black Sleep*. Although mostly identified with the horror roles described in this book, he probably made as many westerns, if not more, including *High Noon*.

Testimony is divided on Creighton as a person. Many who knew him remember a lovable, affable, regular guy, friendly, fun, and unpretentious. Ilona Massey called him, "One of the nicest, sweetest people in the world." Beverly Garland spoke lovingly of him, Elena Verdugo remembers him "with warmth." Patricia Morrison still speaks of him as a "charmer." Peter Coe became one of his best friends.

But others remember a drunken bully boy, boorish, with his own jock-level forms of sadism. Evelyn Ankers wrote of her dislike for him in their numerous movies together, and of the nasty pranks she said he played on her. Jack Pierce disliked him so much that by *House of Dracula*, he refused to make him up, and fobbed him off on an assistant. Bela Lugosi disliked him, but then, disliking actors with better roles than his was Bela's stock-in-trade. Nevertheless, even Karloff never snuck up behind Bela and hoisted him aloft in the air when he was 73, frail from drug rehab, and suffering from heart disease. It's doubtful that Maria Montez was too amused when Creighton pelted feces at the shingle with her name on it on her star bungalow, as reported by Siodmak in his autobiography.

Siodmak also contributes the most off-the-wall comment of all regarding Creighton. Gregory William Mank quotes Siodmak thusly, "His father dominated him to the end of his days, endangering his masculinity. ... Though he raised children and was married to an understanding wife, Lon was sexually confused...he could not adjust to a sexual preference he was unable to accept." Now no one likes to uncover the secret gay lives of old stars more than I do, but I must emphasize that *no one else* I have interviewed or read has *ever* even *hinted* at such an unlikely character trait for Creighton.

What no one denies was that Creighton was a drunk. During the horror revival of the 1960s, American International Pictures brought Karloff, Peter Lorre, and Basil Rathbone back to co-star with the divine Vincent Price, and they each made multiple pictures for the company. Creighton was also brought back by them to share Roger Corman's quite excellent *The Haunted Palace* with Price. Chaney's drab performance brings little to the party besides his name on the marquee. After a while, he just disappears from the movie, with no wind-up for his story arc at all, as though they had failed to get, or had just given up trying to get, the scenes they needed from him, and he made no other pictures for them, though he outlived Karloff, Lorre, and Rathbone, and continued to take whatever acting work he could get up until two years before his death.

He died, predictably from liver disease, on July 12, 1973. I prefer to join with those who remember him fondly. He was neither the first nor the last person to find that the liquor he consumed had consumed him. His beast within had eaten him alive.

24

BAD MOONS ARISIN'

Frankenstein Meets the Wolfman (1943)
House of Frankenstein (1944)
House of Dracula (1945)

(Just the Wolfman bits)

> *Even a man who is pure in heart*
> *And says his prayers by night,*
> *May become a wolf when the wolfbane blooms,*
> *And the moon is full and bright.*
>
> — Curt Siodmak's werewolf doggerel,
> slightly revised to include the full moon

Frankenstein Meets the Wolfman is explicitly set four years after the death of Larry Talbot, which would make it 1945, although it's the oddest 1945 I've ever seen. What happened to cars? What happened to World War II?

Under a full moon, two grave robbers (the doomed one played by the terrific actor Cyril Delevanti) break into the Talbot family crypt, intending to rob the corpse of Lawrence Stewart Talbot. Bad idea. When they open Larry's coffin, they find him packed in wolfsbane, undecomposed, and shortly, under the reviving rays of the full moon, awake again, and his version of horny. One of the grave robbers gets away; Cyril becomes the Wolfman's bitch.

The next morning Larry is found unconscious, with the nasty head wound his father gave him four years earlier bleeding freshly. (Wounds don't heal when you're dead.) Talbot was happy in his coffin, but he now comes to realize that for a wolfman, dying is more complex than it seemed at first. After a couple days in, not surprisingly, "Queen's Hospital," spent convincing Dr. Mannering (who bears an amazing resemblance to Evelyn Ankers' fiance in *The Wolf Man* on account of their both being played by Patric Knowles), a nurse who looks just like one of the locals who shunned him in the last movie (both played by Doris Lloyd), and a local Cardiff constable who bears an amazing resemblance to Basil Rathbone's Inspector Lestrade (Dennis Hoey, giving the exact same performance he gave in the Sherlock Holmes films), that he's insane, Talbot seeks out wizened old Maleva, who comes up with the odd idea that Dr. Frankenstein can help him. This is the first we've heard that Frankenstein's research into life and death included a werewolf catch-and-release program. They take a horsecart to Visaria, as there seem to be no cars, coaches, nor railroads in Europe.

It's a full moon when they arrive in Visaria, so Larry has one of his episodes, killing future star Martha Vickers. When he wakes up after his wolf bender, he's in an ice cave where he finds the Frankenstein Monster frozen in a block of ice.

And that folks, is where we came in.

We are in the *House of Frankenstein* once more. When last seen, Larry Talbot was being washed away by the flood unleashed by a dynamited dam while tussling with the Frankenstein Monster, in the ruins of Ludwig Frankenstein's castle in Visaria.

Gustav Niemann and Daniel the lovesick hunchback arrive at the village of Frankenstein, fresh from abandoning Count Dracula, where they find the even-more-ruined ruins of Castle Frankenstein and a broken dam, which rather curiously have been moved here from Visaria.

At the village, the movie introduces a romantic triangle between Daniel the hunchback, Ilonka the gypsy dancing girl, and the Wolfman. Lovely Elena Verdugo, who plays Ilonka, is only 19 in the movie. We first see her dancing and then, after a financial dispute, we see her being cruelly flogged, or we *try* to, anyway, as when the whipping begins, some old gypsy woman comes and stands right in front of the camera, rudely blocking our view, and *ruining* the movie for the S&M fanciers in the audience. Fortunately, Daniel throttles the whip master and then flogs him, of which we have a slightly better view. Daniel and Gustav take Ilonka away with them. How kind of these two soft-hearted serial murderers.

Daniel immediately falls in love with Ilonka, which in a movie this short with this many plotlines, is a real time saver. When she gets a gander at Daniel's hump, her reaction stops just short of actually vomiting on him. Rude little thing. He stopped her flogging, but she hasn't the manners to conceal her revulsion at his little posture problem. She's not good enough for Daniel. I hope she falls in love with a werewolf.

So Gustav and Daniel find the monster and Larry Talbot frozen in the ice under the ruined ruins. Glancing at the Talbotsicle, Gustav says, "The Wolfman." Not "A wolfman," nor even "A werewolf," but "*The* Wolfman." Gustav knows a celebrity werewolf when he sees one.

Larry drives the wagons to Visaria. He should know the way, having driven Maleva there in the last movie. Ilonka rides up front with him, forming an inexplicable crush on the morose, brooding bruiser, despite his freezing rudeness. "Now don't start barking at me," she says to him in what I hope was an intentional joke.

Larry has become a nag. He repeats variations on "Kill me! Kill me!" more often than Lois Lane in a room full of gangsters. When Gustav tells him he has to wait to die, Larry pumps out his old refrain, "The moon will be full tonight. You know what that means. I can't stand to go through that torture again. I tell you, *I can't!*" With Larry Talbot, it's always all about him. Guess what, Lar. This movie is not titled *House of Wolfman*.

Once Ilonka realizes that Larry really is a werewolf, she confronts him about his down-low existence. He tells her, "Only death can bring us peace of mind." "*Us*"? Hang on a minute there, Fido. *You're* the werewolf. I'm a gypsy dancing girl. I have options. There's a homicidal hunchback who is just nuts for me. Call me Esmeralda.

But in the end, Ilonka proves to be a very understanding girlfriend. She shows her deep love for Talbot by killing him. She puts a lot of work into making herself a silver bullet, displaying smelting and metallurgical skills. She also dies herself, of no perceptible wounds. Gustav, examining her invisible injuries, diagnoses, "The Wolfman." He's a hell of a doctor.

So now Larry is dead, killed by a silver bullet, "fired by the hand of one who loves him enough to understand," a new rule just added for this movie. So he's dead forever, right? Sorry, Lar. This sad excuse for a movie made a lot of money, and Talbot would be back again shortly.

Ten minutes into *House of Dracula*, Lawrence Talbot shows up at Dr. Franz Edelmann's Clinic for the Gender Preference Realignment of Monsters, demanding to see him at once. How is it that Larry is alive again? They don't say. Maybe Ilonka's bullet was only silver plated. Why is he now wearing a natty mustache? Gay clone look?

When the doctor can't see him instantly, he complains of no time and runs off. Sure enough, he waited for a full moon to seek help. Maybe if he'd come by the day before, it wouldn't be so urgent. Perhaps if he'd phoned ahead and made an appointment, like non-lycanthrope patients.

By the time Edelmann's assistant Miliza tells the doctor that a Lawrence Talbot was there to see him, she's clearly already developed feelings for him, despite the fact that she's dating Dracula.

Edelmann and Miliza get a call from Police Inspector Holtz, played by Lionel Atwill, to come to the Visarian police station. Talbot has shown up and demanded to be locked in a cell until dawn. The moon rises, and Edelmann, Miliza, and Holtz all witness the transformation. Locked up and insufficiently superstrong to break out, Larry can't score with anyone. (Fifteen years later, Oliver Reed's wolfman in Hammer films' *The Curse of the Werewolf*, finding himself in the same situation, has no difficulty in pulling the cell door off and throwing it at the constable, to the relief of his terrified cell mate.) Larry's body count *as a werewolf* will be zero in this movie, for Breen Office reasons, though Larry Talbot not in a werewolf state will end a couple lives.

The next day, Larry has his consultation at the clinic, where his curse is X-rayed. I must share the absurd diagnosis with you: "Pressure upon certain parts of the brain. This condition, coupled with your belief that the moon can bring about a change, accomplishes exactly that. ... When this happens, the glands generate an abnormal supply of certain hormones, in your case, those which bring about the physical transformation which you experience." So it's all in his head. Like at puberty, hormones make hair sprout out of his face, change his nose into a dog snout, *and back again*! So when these hormones go, they cause all that wolf hair to retreat back into his face, except for the natty mustache? An operation using mold to soften his skull and enlarge his cranial cavity is the recommended treatment.

Someone has a soft skull, I suspect screenwriter Edward T. Lowe. So how does pressure on the brain account for the way he keeps surviving death?

Dracula, out of maliciousness, reverses a transfusion and gives Dr. Edelmann some of his blood. This should make Edelmann a vampire, but instead it unleashes his beast within, creating a Mr. Hyde semi-transformation. Maybe pressure on his brain is unleashing hormones. Maybe Dracula slipped him some of Larry Talbot's blood. Maybe Edward T. Lowe is just a sloppy writer. Edelmann's transformations are not tied to the moon or to a serum or anything. Whenever the plot needs it, Edelmann changes into a homicidal maniac.

After Larry's operation, Miliza tells Larry that soon he'll love the nights. Larry says, "Until that time comes, I'll live a thousand hopes; die a thousand times." He's severely overestimated the number of sequels still to come.

At his window, Larry sees Edelmann depart with another assistant, Siegfried, on his cart. Bad blood has unleashed Edelmann's inner homo, and he comes on to Siegfried, who has an attack of homosexual panic. Edelmann kills him to keep Siegfried from outing him to all of Visaria. Stupidly, he commits the murder in front of the mob at town hall. (Really, "How To Commit Murder, Lesson #1," is: "Do *not* commit murder in front of a crowd of people.") There's a cool foot chase back to the clinic, with Edelmann holding his wrists at an effeminate angle as he runs, just to look extra sissified.

When the mob, led by Inspector Holtz, arrive, Edelmann has changed back, so they don't recognize him as the killer, even though he looks just like the killer, except except for messy hair and smeared mascara. Edelmann alibis Talbot, and

Talbot repays him by not fingering him for the killing. The down-low beast within boys must stick together.

In explaining his own condition to Talbot, Edelmann makes it all explicit, "My soul and my body have been seized by some nameless horror, a *lust* which changes me." Well, that horror isn't nameless, is it? It's our old friend, lust. There's the name of our beast within, gay or straight: lust.

The moment of truth is fast approaching. The full moon is about to rise. Is Larry cured or isn't he? *He is!* Enlarging his cranial cavity has removed the supernatural curse from him. His hypothalamus now has room to grow to the size of a heterosexual's, and he can live happily ever after with Miliza, who broke up with Dracula when he died anyway.

As Talbot exits the House of Edelmann with Miliza, he looks back to see the monster die in the obligatory conflagration. It happens to be a shot lifted from *Ghost of Frankenstein*, so Talbot is watching himself (and/or Eddie Parker) die.

Dracula and the monster are now dead, with the Wolfman cured. It's all over, right? Sort of, but there was a last, glorious farewell movie coming, and it will be my goodbye as well.

NICE DOGGIE

In *House of Dracula*, the Wolfman never kills anyone. The first time he transforms, he's in a jail cell and can't get his paws on a victim. The second time he changes, he attacks Edelmann, but the moon sets in the nick of time, and he changes back before he can do anything Edelmann might regret. Why?

Since Larry Talbot, a character conceived by Siodmak as someone right out of a Greek tragedy, was this time scheduled for a happily-ever-after ending, the Breen Office decreed that he couldn't kill anyone this time out, because murderers in movies were not allowed to live a happily ever after, as they often do in real life. Of course, the murders he's committed weren't his fault, so he remains a moral innocent, and there is the question of all the people he killed in the previous three movies. Apparently, the movie statute of limitations on werewolf killings expires when each movie ends. Well, if Joseph Breen weren't an idiot, he could never have become a movie censor.

And in the climax of *House of Dracula*, Larry Talbot, while not a werewolf, kills his benefactor Dr. Edelmann and the Frankenstein Monster. The only thing that was consistent in the Breen Office was their inconsistency.

THE BEAST WITHIN QUIZ

(33% of your grade. Answers at the back of the book.)

1. What did Jack Pierce use for the fur on the Wolfman's face?

2. How did the werewolf in Hammer's 1960 *Curse of the Werewolf* acquire his curse?

3. Tom Conway of *Cat People* and *I Walked with a Zombie* was the younger brother of a much more famous actor. Who? Conway narrated what classic Walt Disney animated feature? What was Conway's last movie?

4. Prior to heading RKO's B-unit, Val Lewton was the production supervisor for what legendary film producer?

5. Not counting stunt doubles, Lon Chaney Jr. was the only actor to play Larry Talbot. (At least until the recent remake with Benicio Del Toro.) What other classic Universal monster was only played by a single actor?

EPILOGUE: WHO'S ON LAST?
Abbott & Costello Meet Frankenstein (1948)

Now that we've seen the last of Dracula, the Wolfman, and the monster, there's nobody to frighten us anymore.
— Chick Young (Bud Abbott), being naive

A lot of things were over by 1946. The Great Depression, from which the monsters of the 1930s had diverted audiences, was long gone. World War II, whose anxieties the monsters of the 1940s had relieved, was over. And the Universal Studios that had made them was over as well. In 1946, it was sold yet again, and became the wonderfully redundant Universal-International, headed by pretentious William Goetz, son-in-law of Louis B. Mayer, and held in contempt by the old MGM bastard. Goetz had decreed an end to the monsters.

Abbott & Costello, the great burlesque-vaudeville-Broadway comedy team, had made even more money for the studio during the war than the monsters had, but they hadn't had a hit in a couple of years, and Goetz's contempt for them matched his scorn for the creatures. Classy, high-culture dramas were to be the new Universal-International product, as exemplified by the soon-to-be released *Black Narcissus*, David Lean's *Great Expectations*, and Laurence Olivier's *Hamlet*, which won the Oscar for Best Picture. (Shakespeare was not nominated for his screenplay. *Hamlet* also contained Christopher Lee and Peter Cushing, so the future Hammer Films version of Karloff and Lugosi, Cushing and Lee, first shared a movie for Universal.) Now these were all fine highbrow films, but the studio was soon verging on bankruptcy yet again. Mayer was amused.

By 1948, the studio desperately needed something that would sell tickets, and so when producer Robert Arthur came up with the idea to combine the studio's biggest former money-makers into a single cinematic epic, Goetz gave it a go-ahead, provided they left him alone. He refused even to read the script.

Lou Costello did read the script and hated it. Believe it or not, Abbott & Costello considered the monsters beneath them. Even after the film came out and was a huge hit, one of the top ten grossing movies of the year and one of the studio's top three money-earners for that year, with many a fine review as well, they still disliked it. Even though it re-established them as top movie stars and gave their careers a much-needed second wind, they disdained it.

When I interviewed Bud Abbott in his home in November 1972, and recklessly ventured the opinion that it was their best movie, Bud instantly refuted the heresy, insisting that their best picture was "the army picture." And maybe Bud was right, in that *Buck Privates* is possibly the best *pure* Abbott & Costello movie, but I maintain *Abbott & Costello Meet Frankenstein* is the best overall movie they were ever in. In any event, the years and its popularity failed to impress Bud Abbott. He still had little regard for it.

Abbott & Costello Meet Frankenstein is a clever, funny picture that uses the monsters as straight men to the comics, rather than as buffoons themselves.

A Mr. McDougal, a spiritual descendant of Professor Lampini, has acquired the remains of Dracula and the Frankenstein Monster for his Florida house of horrors, and Chick Young (Bud Abbott) and Wilbur Gray (Lou Costello), a gay couple trying to pass for straight, are the hapless shipping clerks who lose the exhibits. Jane Randolph, the slutty husband-stealing Alice of *Cat People*, is Joan Raymond, the insurance investigator sent to find them.

Of course, Dracula and Frankenstein aren't dead (are they ever this early in a movie?), and have wandered off after Chick and Wilbur unpacked them in a sweet comic set-piece, which included reading aloud signs that give a quick run down of who the monsters are, what their powers are, etc. This was the first

Universal monster movie I ever saw, and that quick refresher course on the monsters was my introduction to them.

Lugosi has finally, after 17 years, returned to the role of Dracula. The studio insanely felt that the sixty-five-year-old Bela was *too old* to play the *400-year-old* Count Dracula. If anything, he was too young. These people were not geniuses, however much they bragged of making (actually, only releasing) *Hamlet*.

Count Dracula has his own agenda going. He wants the monster for his hunky boy toy. (The movie never explains what the hell Count Dracula needs with the Frankenstein Monster in the first place, so I'm free to assume his motivation for myself.) However, Dracula knows that the brain in the monster's head is dangerously evil. He should know. As the attentive reader recalls, it's Lugosi's own brain, since it's still Ygor's old brain, considerably the worse for a lot of wear. Dracula wants a fresh, pliable brain in the monster, and has enlisted dubious scientist Dr. Mornay, played by the lovely Lenore Aubert, to choose a suitable brain and transplant it into the monster's square skull.

Dr. Mornay, being a scientist, naturally has her own gigantic gothic castle, on an island in the Everglades, which, as everyone knows, is rife with castles. There she lives with her blandly handsome assistant Dr. Stevens, in whom she shows not the faintest interest, so we can assume she's a lesbian if we want to, and I do. She pretends a romantic interest in Wilbur Gray, but that's just to acquire his, for want of a better word, brain. Joan Raymond also pretends to have the hots for short, tubby, dumb Wilbur, to get him to lead her to the missing monsters. Wilbur, being a man, believes both women are hot for him.

Who should also show up but Larry Talbot, of course. His cure has worn off. I guess his skull hardened up, and his glands went nuts once again. Milizia, his love interest from *House of Dracula*, is neither seen nor mentioned, like a Bond girl come the next movie. Talbot is trailing Dracula, having appointed himself the Monster Police, determined to put an end to Dracula and the monster before they can reunite again for *House of Wolfman*. Plus, he's apparently over his death wish. He does trot out the horror staple of demanding Wilbur lock him in his room for the night.

They keep the plot advancing, yet find time for a number of perfectly brought off comedy set pieces. Wilbur sitting on the monster's lap without noticing. (Glenn Strange had a particularly hard time shooting this scene. Out-take footage of Strange repeatedly laughing during the sequence exists.) Larry changing into a werewolf as he is trying to unstrap Wilbur from an operating table. Dracula attending a masquerade party costumed as Dracula.

The primary running gag is that only Wilbur ever sees the monsters alive. Whenever he tries to show them to Chick, they are missing in action. It's amazing how long they keep that one gag percolating without it ever lapsing into being annoying. There are lots of good quotable jokes:

> Talbot: In half an hour the moon will rise, and I'll turn into a wolf.
> Wilbur: You and twenty million other guys.
>
> ---
>
> Dracula: You young people, making the most of life, *while it lasts.*
>
> ---
>
> Chick: I wish you'd stop trying to put those ideas into this boy's head. He's not used to them.
>
> ---
>
> Wilbur: "Frankie, I'm tellin' ya, it's a bad deal. I've had this brain for thirty years and it hasn't worked right yet." (Lou Costello must have had a brain transplant when he was around twelve years old, because he was forty-two when he delivered this line.)

Chaney carries much of the picture quite well. He's ceased to be the self-pitying whiner he'd been for the last three movies. Lugosi is excellent in his comic take on Dracula, and Glenn Strange has more to do as the monster than in both of the last two movies combined. He even has a few lines. OK, all he ever says is, "Yes, Master," but I've gotten through entire weekends of pleasant fun while only using those two words. It was, by all accounts, a happy, fun set, with lots of onset pranks and gags (some of these are preserved in its out-takes also), and only humorless Lugosi was put off by the air of undisciplined joking going on.

The climax is a farcical, slapstick free-for-all chase around the castle and its grounds. Chaney did put on the monster costume and make-up to double for Strange tossing Dr.

EPILOGUE: WHO'S ON LAST?

Mornay out a window after Glenn had broken his foot on a previous attempt.

And then, at long, long last, the monsters meet their final ends. Dracula, transforming into a bat, is grabbed by the Wolfman, and they both plunge to the rocks and water below, while the monster is set ablaze (again) on a pier. None of these deaths should work. A fall into water and rocks would not faze Dracula nor the Wolfman, both of whom have survived worse, while the monster falls through the burning pier into the water, just as he had at the beginning of *Bride of Frankenstein*. Perhaps the fire mellowed out Ygor's old brain and he became affable dolt Herman Munster.

Yet these *are* their ultimate, final deaths. Seventeen years of gay monster fun is over. The Universal creatures had had their last hurrah, or last arrrrggggh. It is a glorious last hurrah. It is a vastly better movie on all levels than any of them had been in in six or seven years. But the threats to society must finally die. Only the respectably partnered male couple of Bud & Lou survive, to finish off the Mummy, the Invisible Man, and Jekyll & Hyde in the movies this one spawned.

The curtain gag in *Abbott & Costello Meet Frankenstein* also gave an unintentional hint of what lay ahead. Chick and Wilbur are paddling away from the castle in a rowboat. As they chat, they fail to notice a cigarette lighting and smoking itself. Chick says, "Oh, relax. Now that we've seen the last of Dracula, the Wolfman, and the monster, there's nobody to frighten us anymore."

A strangely familiar, silky voice says, "Oh, that's too bad. I was hoping to get in on the excitement."

"Who said that?" barks Chick.

"Allow me to introduce myself," the voice continues. "I'm the Invisible Man."

As he laughs maniacally, Chick and Wilbur jump overboard and swim for shore. (It's the Florida Everglades. I hope they didn't encounter any alligators or water moccasins.)

The uncredited voice of the Invisible Man belonged to Vincent Price. Five years later he would make *House of Wax*, and rise from character actor to horror star. Seven years after that, he would make *House of Usher*, and become the great

American horror icon of the 1960s, providing the effete, sexually ambiguous charm to the upcoming horror movies of the next generation, balancing the no-nonsense butch manliness of the other two new icons, Peter Cushing and Sir Christopher Lee. Additionally, Price would appear with Karloff, Chaney, Rathbone, and Lorre, seeing them through their final horrors, riding the crest of the new wave of color shockers that would come to theaters just as the Universal classics hit TV, and a generation of "monster kids," myself one of them, fell in love with the older movies and the new. Vincent was horror's future. But his great tale is for another day.

For I can hear my cock crow now. The sky is growing light in the east. It's time for me to repair to my crypt and close the lid on my bed until another day. Thank you for sharing this journey with me. I have time for just one more word.

Boo!

APPENDIX
Quiz Answers

The Living Dead Quiz Answers

1. The manager of the Lyceum Theater in London's West End for Sir Henry Irving, the greatest English star of his day, and many say, the inspiration for Stoker's Count Dracula.

2. Oscar Wilde. Given the homosexual sex scandal that sent him to prison in disgrace, I'd say Florence made the right choice.

3. The 1922 German silent *Nosferatu: A Symphony of Horror*. Clearly based on Stoker's novel, Murnau hadn't bothered to acquire the film rights. Mrs. Stoker sued for copyright violation and won. She insisted on a judgment of total extinction for the movie. Every copy was to be found and burned. Given what a creepy masterpiece it is, we are very lucky she failed to find *all* the prints.

4. Ian Keith, who played the evil Rochefort in the MGM version of *The Three Musketeers*, a role played by Christopher Lee in the Michael York / Richard Lester remake. Keith's evil boss, Cardinal Richelieu, was played by Vincent Price.

5. In the 1959 Hammer remake, the mummy was Christopher Lee, and the hero was Peter Cushing. In the 1999 Universal remake, hunky South African actor Arnold Vosloo played the mummy as a shirtless muscle stud (necrophilia has never looked so good), and the hero was gorgeous Brendan Fraser.

The Mad Science Quiz Answers

1. Mary Wallstonecroft Godwin Shelley.

2. *A Vindication of the Rights of Women* by Mary Wallstonecroft. Women's rights.

3. In 1957, Hammer made *The Curse of Frankenstein*. The monster was Christopher Lee, and Baron Victor Frankenstein was Peter Cushing. (In 1970, Hammer remade their own film, turning *The Curse of Frankenstein* into *Horror of Frankenstein*, doing it as a subtle send-up, with David "Darth Vader" Prowse as a shirtless muscle hunk of a monster and Ralph Bates as Victor Frankenstein.) In 1994, in *Mary Shelley's Frankenstein*, Victor Frankenstein was Kenneth Branagh, who also directed, while the monster was Robert DeNiro with the brain of John Cleese. (How bad an idea was that?)

4. According to make-up artist Jack Pierce, he designed the monster with a flat head because his "research" showed that a hinged, flat skull would be easiest to open and close when swapping brains. James Whale also claimed he had designed the flat-head look as well, for the same reason. Where they were able to research flat skulls, I do not know. Where Henry Frankenstein found a flat-headed skull, I do not know. What I do know is that if you are going to transplant a brain, most of your most delicate work will be below the brain, attaching it to the spinal cord, not from its pop-up skull top.

5. American-International Pictures' (no relation to Universal-International) *The Comedy of Terrors*, directed by *Cat People*'s Jacques Tourneur and written by Richard Matheson. It was released in 1964, and I have a deep indefensible love for it.

APPENDIX: QUIZ ANSWERS

The Beast Within Quiz Answers

1. Yak fur.

2. Oliver Reed's sexy werewolf's father was a beggar who was confined in a cage with dogs for decades by a cruel Spanish aristocrat, until he was bestial himself. He raped Oliver's mother, and the child of rape, fathered by a man-dog, and born on Christmas Day (considered an insult to God, which is bad news for everyone with a Christmas birthday) is therefore cursed to turn into a werewolf whenever his baser emotions are aroused, as they were rather regularly. He's even more innocent than Larry Talbot. He was "born that way."

3. George Sanders. *Walt Disney's Peter Pan*. *What a Way to Go*, also the final film of comedy legend Margaret Dumont.

4. David O. Selznick.

5. No other monster was only played by a single actor.

ABOUT THE AUTHOR

Douglas McEwan is the author of three comic novels all dealing with motion pictures, actors and Hollywood, *My Lush Life*, *Tallyho, Tallulah!*, and, also available from Pulp Hero Press, *My Gruesome Life*. In the 1970s he wrote the Los Angeles TV program *Fright Night with Seymour*, his scripts for which were collected and published in *Creatures of the Night That We Loved So Well: The Horror Hosts of Southern California* (Second Edition) by James Fetters. In 1974 he wrote and co-produced the "Seymour's Halloween Haunt" stage show at Knott's Berry Farm. In 1976, his serious full-length stage adaptation of *Dracula* was produced in Los Angeles. He has worked as an actor, a comedy writer, and a comedian on stage, radio, and television. He lives in Los Angeles with two cats who think they're scary. They're not.

Printed in Great Britain
by Amazon